COLIN SCOTT

IT DOESN'T TAKE A BRAIN TUMOUR

Pulling Down the Stronghold of False Religion

COLIN SCOTT

It Doesn't Take a Brain Tumour

Pulling Down the Stronghold of False Religion

*There is a vast difference
between repeating
what you believe,
and believing
what you repeat.*

THANK YOU

Far above, name above all names, Jesus! Thank you, Lord, for laying down Your life for me. May I continue to grow in knowing You and who I am in You. You are truth. Seeking to know the truth is seeking to know You. I pray that more people, in their pursuit to find the truth, find You.

There are a few key people that I want to mention here.

John Kinghorn - My friend for many years, who has been more involved in contending for my healing than anyone I know. Who, since hospital, is the person closest to me, who believes most as I do. A man seeking to let Christ be shown in his life, and is a blessing to all who cross his path.

James Dean and Jared Hunt. Out of all the people that came to pray for me in hospital, these two were the only ones that I remember who came in and prayed for me, 100% convinced that the trial I was facing was not God's doing, and now I agree.

Joel Devcich and Rachael Marquet. My friends who have most consistently checked in on me and seek to encourage me in my pressing on.

Geoff Winter - What can God do with a man who just says yes? One of the wrong mindsets we face today is, "have a go". Geoff personifies the mindset of GET IT DONE!

My home group. For seeking to know the truth with me, not just a way that seems right; praying with me, supporting and challenging me, helping me to bring the Kingdom near people.

To my editor Colleen. You have been very helpful and encouraging in the process of getting my book together. You were great to work with.

Three awesome men from the States whom I have followed online. Curry Blake, Andrew Womack, and Dan Mohler. These three have had a significant influence on my life in both truth and love.

My amazing wife, Kelly, and family, who continue to love and support me. I love you heaps and hope to live in a way that releases more and more of the fullness of God in our lives.

FROM THE AUTHOR

This book is in your hands because I genuinely believe and prophesy that it will multiply truth, grace and peace in your life, that it would sōzō[1] you and others.

It is written to highlight the difference between what seems right to man trying to reason their experience and what God says, then to encourage you to believe the latter.

I know that God has been speaking to me as I have diligently sought the truth of who He is and who I am in Christ.

This book will result in bringing people to Christ! Whether it encourages closeness, enables people to be more effective witnesses, or gives a much clearer understanding of who He is that people want to draw near to.

Renewing my mind with the truth has greatly multiplied freedom in my life and has resulted in producing much of God's fruit.

If you discover this book has impacted you for good, please commit to helping me spread it to others.

---

[1] Strong's G4982 - σῴζω - (sode'-zo)
  sózó: to save, rescue

FOREWORD

The book you hold in your hands is a must-read for all those disillusioned by a religious system that has buried so many in tombs of rituals, dead works, confusion, and unbelief. Colin's down-to-earth approach and writing style as he pulls down religious strongholds, should breathe new life into your faith journey and, by God's grace, call you back to your first love for the Word of God and an intimate relationship with Jesus Christ as your Lord God, Healer, Deliverer and Saviour!

Insights Colin has gained as he wrestled with his belief systems in the face of a brain tumour, will empower you to find a new platform of faith, ready to stand strong in the face of the storms of life.

Invite Holy Spirit to work with you as you allow each chapter to challenge you and strengthen you in the truth, for surely, "the truth will set you free" and bring you into new seasons of freedom in Christ. Happy reading!

Pastor/ Evangelist Geoff Winter.

Manifest Love Church, Hamilton.

Contents

INTRODUCTION

You might have heard it said that some things don't take a rocket scientist or a brain surgeon, but you've probably never heard, "it doesn't take a brain tumour."

While lying in hospital, diagnosed with a brain tumour in early 2020, I realised I didn't actually know what I believed. I could recite what religion said and quote what seemed right to man, but what was right? What is truth?

My main purpose in writing this book is to show people familiar with Christian religion, as I was, the vast difference between what God says and what 'false' religion says. Our reasoning may 'seem right,' 'sound good,' or 'get us through,' but it could render God's Word useless (Mark 7:13) and stop us from living the life that Jesus paid so much for. I quickly discovered that I didn't know what I truly believed after decades of Christian religion.

I came out of hospital with a desire to know what God said because I knew man's word wouldn't save me. I knew I had (*have*) eternal life, but did God want me healed on earth? If He did, what was my part to play in receiving it? Could I bring healing to others?

Trying to answer these questions set me on a course of seeking to know the truth at the expense of my previous experience and understanding. This was a purposeful, intentional journey.

This book is mainly broken into three different sections. Firstly, a pulling down part, in which I talk about wrong believing, strongholds, and how strongholds are made. These are things that I believe actually affect your living and relationship with the Father. In these sections, I show what scripture says and how different that is to some of the believing false religion strengthens.

In the testimony sections, I talk about how my life has been changed as a result of pulling down strongholds and changing my believing. I share blessings I have had from allowing God's word to have effect in my life. Although I don't always understand (Philippians 3:14), more fruit comes from pressing on believing His Word than leaning on any understanding.

In the building up sections, I highlight what the Word says you should believe. In these parts, I encourage you to believe God's Word, to trust Him, stand in faith, act and persevere in His Word, especially when the circumstances you fall into look nothing like His Word.

I pray that as you continue reading, you will learn some truths you should know without God having to make good out of a brain-tumour-like situation.

ONE

CAN I GET THAT IN WRITING?

Playing guitar became difficult.

I would like to start this book by stating very clearly that what I say is not important, except when it is aligned with God's Word, then I say it with all my heart, soul, mind, and strength.

This chapter contains some information about my life. It's not an attempt to gain sympathy but to show you why I am so passionate about knowing and sharing the truth.

My life before being diagnosed with a brain tumour, was much like many people's—family, friends, work, hobbies, and church. I always tried to be nice and apologised when I wasn't. I celebrated achievements, struggled with stuff, and lent a hand to people who asked. I occasionally prayed about things and sporadically read my Bible, but I was much more interested in meeting the church's needs. It felt as though I prayed more on stage than off, in my role as a worship leader, and memorising Scripture was only to help me pray better-sounding prayers. Who was I trying to please?

I was much more interested in meeting the church's needs

I served in my church gathering (and others) to meet any creative need I could be busy with. Whether it was crawling under a stage to adjust cables or leading the singing, it didn't matter, although I probably only had a limited amount of grace for cobwebs. I mostly played guitar and led the singing, but I did everything else, from drums to controlling the lights.

When things went well, I praised God; when things were hard, I praised God. Being a 'good' Christian seemed to be how prone you were to praise God despite what life threw at you.

Symptoms of my eventual diagnosis seemed to start way back in 2015 when I started feeling quite nauseous after attending an overseas conference. It was my first time out of the country, so anxiety or other issues could have been expected. But when it kept occurring, I decided to see a doctor. I did all the required tests, and it was decided that I had IBS (Irritable Bowel Syndrome). This is medical language for, *"something is upsetting your stomach, but we don't know what."* Anxiety toward food grew into a huge issue for me, but when the doctor gave me this diagnosis, I had confidence to allow it to continue, thinking the worst that might happen was losing my lunch. I believed at the time, that if God allowed it to happen, it was ok. God knew best, and I would still praise Him.

The next thing that happened was my knee becoming sore. That led me to buy better running shoes, but that didn't fix the problem; it just seemed to move it to my hip. I never considered it was related to the issues with my gut. After this continued for some time, a new person joined our church who, on several occasions, spoke to my knee and told it to heal and recover. I believe it did at times, only to find the pain would soon return.

I started getting headaches more frequently, but my body was under some stress, so that was to be expected. I wondered if any of it was related to eye strain, so I explored that and got some glasses, but that didn't seem to help, so I kept taking painkillers and pressed on.

Then everything changed for me when my guitar started getting harder to play. I continued on for a few weeks, blaming my tools (my guitar). Then it dawned on me that my guitar was perfectly fine, but the arm that was finding it difficult to hold the strings, was on the same side of the body as my weak and pained leg.

There is so much more to the drama I faced, and looking at it summed up like this, it's easy to think, "Why didn't he work it out sooner?" But this happened over a few years, and it didn't occur to me at the time that any of this was related.

I started to pray a little more then, but my body didn't change, so I kept praising God and being nice. If God wasn't going to heal me divinely, then regardless of His will, I was going back to man; back to the medical system.

I wonder if, when someone prays for healing, and it doesn't happen instantly, they conclude that God doesn't want them to be healed, so they obey His will and choose to stay unwell?

On Valentine's Day of 2020, I was finally diagnosed with a brain tumour. Weird as this may sound, I was so relieved at first. I now knew my being nauseous so often had nothing to do with eating, and my anxiety toward food stopped immediately.

I would like to say that this was all that happened to my body, but unfortunately, not. Two weeks later, I had a biopsy that ended up severely reducing the quality of my life. What was supposed to be a one-hour procedure became six and nearly took my life. It took away the co-ordination of my good side, my ability to drive, caused double vision, numbness in part of my face and mouth, and stole my sense of taste. It completely took away my ability to walk for several weeks.

With so much stolen from me during this time, I still smiled a lot; probably even laughed. I was polite. I definitely enjoyed visits from my wife, family, and friends. I would say I was more positive than half the people who visited. I even tried playing my kids' guitar a few times when I could. Going to church for twenty plus years resulted in me being a reasonably nice person, even when the proverbial rug was pulled out.

The medical system determined they could do nothing for me but only delay what they thought would happen. There are a lot of things that influenced my decision not to proceed with any further treatment from then on. Some people patted me on the back, and it felt like others cut me out of their lives, but I have great peace about my choice.

It was during this time that my belief was finally challenged. When learning to walk again physically, I realised that I needed to learn to walk again spiritually. I didn't really know what God said; I just knew what my religion said. If man says there is nothing they can do, what's left? Die as nicely as you can? I chose to have faith in and stand on God's Word. It turns out that if you are going to stand on God's Word, you need to know what you are standing on. As you learn the truth of what He says, you have much less tolerance for what just 'seems' right.

> *You need to know what you are standing on.*

At this time, it was like someone had turned on a light, and now I could clearly see some things that were making me stumble (Psalms 119:105). Like Hosea 4:6 says, "My people are destroyed for lack of knowledge." Was there knowledge that could stop me from being destroyed? Could the correct knowledge stop destruction in the lives of others?

The answer is, YES!

Imagine walking with God in the cool of the day like Adam and Eve did, not needing a theology or a doctrine about who God is because He could just tell you. Wouldn't that be great? Just the thought of that offers a sense of peace. God telling us who He is. You might be quicker than me on this; it only took a couple of decades for me to realise, this is exactly what the Bible is.

In my life, I had let experience have more sway over how God was described than the Bible. If something seemed right to me, then that was good enough. Just a thought, would you let me tell you who God was, based on how I experienced life? I had. But if Jesus is the same yesterday, today, and forever (Hebrews 13:8), then isn't He who the Bible says He is, regardless of how our life plays out?

Have you ever found yourself saying, "Can I get that in writing?" I imagine many people have had lawyers look over contracts carefully to ensure they know exactly what is said. Imagine the bank calls someone and says they have been selected to have their mortgage paid off in three months. Do you think a phone call is enough evidence?

It seems, in the natural, people would rather have a written word but when it comes to the things of God, I could tell you, "He told me...," and if it sounds reasonable, people won't likely challenge it. Jesus says, "Blessed are you, Simon Peter," in Matthew 16:17, for hearing from the Father, and then six verses later, He says something that seemed right and is accused of speaking the words of satan. So how do we know what is to be believed? The simple answer: it is written!

This book is not the Bible, just in case you were wondering. It is merely an attempt to stir you to believe what is written in God's Word. It has taken me a great deal of effort to ensure there are very few of my thoughts and opinions in the chapters ahead because I don't need you to remember *my* words, but God's. My journey is woven into this writing, but it's only there to encourage you to keep reading. I know there is so much in this book that will bless you.

> *This book… attempts to stir you to believe what is written in God's Word.*

As you read on, I hope I convey things well, help clear the path ahead of you, and give you Biblical knowledge that stops destruction in your life as it has done in mine. Let's start pulling down the strongholds of false religion in our lives!

TWO

BUILDING IN THE STORM

*I am building a new house,
on the rock, but in the storm.*

**Sanctify them by Your truth.
Your word is truth. - John 17:17**

For many years, I devoted myself to ensuring the smooth running of the religious machine. I juggled my roles as a husband, father, employee, and various other commitments to serve in my local meeting place and others. I was undoubtedly driven by the desire to please man and earn God's favour, to be a 'good' Christian. However, in my hospital bed, I realised that I had foolishly built my house (faith) on the sand, despite the many years of being immersed in religion. My beliefs were based on what I had religiously repeated; on what seemed right; on false religion, and not on the Word of God.

I believed all that was happening to me (or being allowed to happen), was to achieve His will that was higher than mine. If God needed my wife to go without a husband, my kids to go without an earthly father, family, friends, church, work, and neighbours to be without me, then who was I to believe anything but 'Thy will be done'? I was willing to accept death and give God the glory, believing that His plan was being accomplished through me.

During that difficult time, my religion (belief structure) provided very little comfort beyond the knowledge that God was still good and to be trusted, despite my circumstances. I felt grateful for the prayers of the many people who came to support me and my family, showing their love and care. But what could they have faith for, besides that I would accept my suffering well, making sure that my sackcloth was on straight? Could they convince God, by their repetitions, to change His mind? Did they think God didn't know the gravity of my situation and would change His plan if He did? I was so troubled, and I couldn't even take refuge in the strong tower because I thought He was the one who was "lovingly" doing this to me.

> *Could they convince God, by their repetitions, to change His mind?*

Jesus said to him, "Have I been with you so long, and yet you have not known Me, Philip? He who has seen Me has seen the Father; so how can you say, 'Show us the Father'?" John 14:9

All of this started to change very quickly when I listened to a song in hospital with the lyrics, "What would you do if He walked in the room?" I realised in a heartbeat that I would simply say, "Thank you." That any suffering I was going through would have just ended. Any excuse for me to stay unwell ceases to make any sense when Christ

> *If Jesus heals someone, is He casting out God to do so?*

walks into the room. He healed all who came to Him. I realised immediately that I believed Jesus to be different from the Father, yet He says, *"if you've seen Me, you've seen the Father."* (John 14:9)

Jesus is the exact representation of God (Hebrews 1:3) and only did what He saw the Father doing (John 5:19). I had believed that Jesus Christ would heal me, but that God the Father would make me sick to accomplish some plan. There's a problem here! I was seeing them very, very differently.

What excuse or lie are you believing which allows Jesus and the Father to look different? Did Jesus ever give someone sickness? No! If Jesus heals someone, is He casting out God to do so; a house divided? I left the hospital declaring that I wanted to know what God said, and I didn't care what seemed right to a man (Proverbs 14:12).

Right relationship with God accomplishes His will on earth (Mark 9:14-29). People seem to prefer questioning His will over whether they're living right. Is it so important to ensure what you believe and how you live is right? Does it even make a difference to how your life plays out? Are you acting or failing to act because of wrong beliefs? Are you deceived? 1 Timothy 4:16 tells us in no uncertain terms that it does have an effect. So how do you know what you believe is the truth? The simple answer: it is what God says. God's Word is truth!

It takes much less effort to build your house in the sand, but it is foolish (Matthew 7:26). Whether your house is on the sand or on the rock, the storm still comes (John 16:33). I had built in the sand, a sand-castle stronghold of false religion that collapsed with the first wave. My house crumbled abruptly, and great was its fall. By God's mercy and grace, I am building a new house on the Rock, but in the storm. If the storm is coming regardless, wouldn't you rather know your house was on the rock before it comes?

> ***"These things I have spoken to you, that in
> Me you may have peace.
> In the world you will have
> tribulation; but be of good cheer,
> I have overcome the world."
> John 16:33***

"Will have" tribulations (storms). This doesn't mean God plans them, makes them, or allows (wants) them, but He knows they'll come. I know you will have troubles without coming to your house and causing them. You don't need to ask for them, but you can "be of good cheer" and have peace in Him during them. You can and should believe right and live right before and during them. What I believed going into the hospital after years of religion, is far from what I believe now.

I am very much aware that people want to have a reason, a purpose for their suffering. They want to have a joy set before them (Hebrews 12:2). When people pray a time or two, and their mountain doesn't seem to move, they tend to conclude that it's God's will. Is it? What amount of resistance makes something a will of God and not just a work of the devil? The answer is that no amount of resistance, large or small, determines what is God's will. Read Mark 9:14-29; Jesus healed the boy. It was still His will regardless of the disciples' failing.

I want to draw your attention to James 1:2, we "fall" into trials.

My brethren, count it all joy when you fall into various trials.
James 1:2

Something that has helped me better understand God's Word was following a suggestion to ask yourself, "what is this verse **not** saying?" People have rewritten James 1:2 to say, "when God takes you through trials to achieve a purpose," which it clearly does not; it says "fall." I pray that one word has already set some people free.

God doesn't have a plan that you fall.

Besides humour, do you know anyone who falls or trips over intentionally to achieve a purpose? It is usually an unplanned thing. If you fall into a snare, a pit, or a hole in the ground, do you think God dug it for you? God does not have trials ahead that we should walk in; He has good works (Ephesians 2:10). God doesn't have a plan that you "fall"; He has a plan not to harm you (Jeremiah 29:11).

When you do "fall" into a trial, you can consider it pure joy for the chance to test your faith (James 1:3). The joy set before you is the opportunity to believe God, not the trial. If you do not choose to believe God, what you're left with is the trial, no joy. Position yourself so that you are ready to receive Him working it out for good. Cooperate with Him by praying His will **be** done. Continue to believe and live in a way that brings Him glory. Press on, loving God and loving people.

So, what do you believe? Is it the truth?
What makes something the will of God?
Are you confident that you are believing correctly
and not just what you have 'religiously' repeated?
I pray you would seek and know the Truth
and build your house on the rock,
before any storm comes.

THREE

STRONGHOLD OF FALSE RELIGION

What are we talking about?

First, what is religion? You could find many definitions on this, but for the purpose of this book, I will define it as: *the way you act in relation to who God is.*

What is false religion then? *Action based on a wrong understanding of who God is.* You will behave very differently depending on who you think God is.

What is a stronghold? *Wrong believing that exalts itself against the knowledge (truth) of God.*

Repetitive actions (habits) will strengthen your beliefs, whether right or wrong, like a well-worn path. If you base the way you live your life on wrong beliefs, allowing them to shape your identity, then this becomes not just what you do but who you are. This makes identifying false beliefs or talking about truth without people feeling attacked or offended (which I have zero desire to do), challenging.

Imagine living for decades believing wrongly, as I did! This became a significant stronghold in my life. It caused me to act or not act due to who I thought God was. Fortunately, Holy Spirit is on our side, encouraging us to pull down strongholds of wrong thinking (2 Corinthians 10:4-5), but we first have to see them for what they are, before we can even desire to pull them down.

One of the first verses that stood out to me when I left hospital was…

> **There is a way that seems right to a man,**
> **But its end is the way of death.**
> **Proverbs 14:12**

I knew a way that seemed right. Do you?

> **Trust in the LORD with all your heart,**
> **And lean not on your own understanding;**
> **Proverbs 3:5**

I was leaning on my own understanding, that I had taken from my religion. Are you?

***Take heed to yourself and to the doctrine.
Continue in them, for in doing this,
you will save both yourself
and those who hear you.
1 Timothy 4:16***

Did I believe correctly after being in church for so long? Surely?

Looking back on my past years of being a Believer, going to church nearly every week, often more than one service, playing and leading worship at different meeting places, even simultaneously, holding and participating in home groups, attending many events and conferences, including one overseas, and going to various training and networking nights, I still didn't know *what* I believed. I could easily repeat what my religion said; I was very familiar with it. I am not someone who just tried being a Christian and then became judgmental of it when things got hard. I lived it 'religiously' for many, many years! I knew what man said, but what good was that to me? I needed to know what **God** said!

Was I facing a trial that required me to stand in faith, in my armour, and resist the enemy, or was it God's will, and I needed to put on some sackcloth? How do we know what God's will is? Is it just what happens? Could we accidentally thank the wrong source for things

(James 1:16)? Could we be angry at God for events in our lives that He had nothing to do with? Was I experiencing a "blessing in disguise?" *Would you have a better relationship with God if He gave you a brain tumour?* I can tell you that I prayed a time or two, and the mountain didn't seem to move. That made it God's will, right? Didn't it? So many questions!

> *Was it God's will, and I needed to put on some sackcloth?*

I can't think of a way, besides a brain tumour, that I could have been made aware of or even desire to pull down a stronghold of false religion in my life. This is how false religion is birthed. I could reason that my experience was all a part of God's design and that this book is only part of His unknowable plan. I could come up with something that seemed right to a man and pass that on to others.

Paul said to Timothy in 1 Timothy 4:16, *"Be mindful, take heed how you live and what you believe, because in doing so you will save (sōzō[2]) both yourself and those who hear you."* Let's make it crystal clear from the start: There is not much you need to know to inherit eternal

---

[2] Strong's G4982 - σῴζω - (sode'-zo)
sózó: to save, rescue

life. All have fallen short and need the redemption of Christ. What else do I need to believe and do besides saying a 'sinner's prayer'?

Do a word study, even right now, on the difference between eternal life in John 3:16 and saved (sōzō) in John 3:17. There is a big difference! If you don't believe me, someone got sōzō in Matthew 9:22 (the same word as in 1 Timothy 2:4 that God desires all men to have) just by touching the hem of His garment. I don't think that's how you get eternal life.

> ***...who desires all men to be saved
> and to come to the knowledge
> of the truth. - 1 Timothy 2:4***

The English word 'saved' is the Greek word 'sōzō'. So, what does God want for us? What is sōzō? A simple definition is: whole, healed, delivered, protected. This is worth studying. As you continue reading, I hope you will discover truth that will save (sōzō) you and others. We don't want worthless religion!

> ***If anyone among you thinks he is
> religious, and does not bridle his tongue
> but deceives his own heart,
> this one's religion is useless.
> James 1:26***

Deception, or calling someone deceived, sounds very judgemental. I have absolutely no desire to judge or condemn anyone. Deception is not a choice to do something wrong, but it is allowing yourself to believe reasoning, a way that seems right to man, in place of what God says is the truth. It's called 'a way that seems right' for a reason. We need to know what *is* right.

Right now, ask yourself, do you desire to know the truth? God desires it. This is something I pray that you want. But as much as I want it for you, it is your choice. I encourage you to pray that the Holy Spirit leads you into it (John 16:13) and sets you free

> *I am not interested in feeling good while being deceived.*

(John 8:32). Not as some might say "my truth" (1 Corinthians 3:18-20), but "the truth" (John 17:17). I am not interested in feeling good while being deceived. Personally, I would prefer not to feel good about believing and doing wrong. I would rather have my feelings challenged while believing and doing right.

- Truth - regardless of who said it.

- Truth - regardless of how it makes you feel.

- Truth - regardless of whether it disagrees with a way that used to seem right.

- Truth - what God says.

Renewing our minds to truth will also renew our actions and bring God's kingdom and His will on earth. I know I was deceived, and God showed me truth that freed me. I pray He speaks truth through me and multiplies your freedom.

Although I know now what I have gone through was not caused by God trying to accomplish some unknowable plan, not a blessing in disguise, not in the least bit His will, I am very grateful for the good He has been doing in it and through it.

I greatly desire to point you to the truth **as it is written** in the Word of God, which I strongly promote, and that my reasoning is ignored. A brain tumour led me to seek God passionately like it was life or death. I hope that my trial will do more than just change my life. God's Word will set you free, not mine. Invite God to speak as you read; otherwise, my words are in vain. Ask Him what He wants you to hear.

Unless the LORD builds the house,
They labour in vain who build it;
Unless the LORD guards the city,
The watchman stays awake in vain.
Psalms 127:1

Lord, may we hear Your words only,
and may my words fall by the way side.
Thank you, that You are with us,
speaking to us through Your Word.
May You sanctify us by Your truth;
Your Word is Truth.

FOUR

PURE AND UNDEFILED RELIGION

What are you doing religiously that contradicts what you believe?

Let's make it super clear from the start. I am not against 'true' religion; I am against 'false' religion which teaches people to believe what God never said and then repeats it until it becomes a stronghold (mindset). Just because something seems right and is repeated, doesn't mean it is right. Repetition **does not** equal truth. His Word is truth. Do you believe God or man?

> ***But Peter and the other apostles answered and said: "We ought to obey God rather than men." - Acts 5:29***

Religion, **true** Christian religion, has its rightful place in our lives. Here are some aspects of the Christian faith that I am for:

- Meeting together (Hebrews 10:25)

- Praising His Holy name (Psalm 103:1)

- Seeking first His kingdom and righteousness on earth (Matthew 6:33)

- Remembering and proclaiming Jesus' death and resurrection, taking the Lord's Supper, discerning His body (Luke 22:19)

- Stirring each other up in the faith and to good works (Hebrews 10:24)

- Iron sharpening iron (Proverbs 27:17)

- Visiting the sick, widows, orphans (James 1:27), and those in prison or being mistreated (Hebrews 13:3)

- Rejoicing in the truth (1 Corinthians 13:6)

- Celebrating Christ in you (Colossians 1:27), and so on...

~PULLING DOWN~

We are instructed to be careful what we believe (1 Timothy 4:16 and Matthew 24:4), but are we so confident that we are not deceived? While in hospital, I realised very quickly that there were many areas in my life where I did not believe what God said, just what *seemed* right.

I was misled, having believed what I religiously repeated. In many ways, I knew I was being destroyed for lack of knowledge (Hosea 4:6). Lies had found their way into my beliefs. I chose to believe people's reasoning of God's Word rather than just believing God's Word. I was deceiving myself and others, conforming to a false religion of useless, ineffective niceness. Dare I say, believing as commandments of God, the doctrines of men and of devils (1 Timothy 4:1). I was worshipping God in vain (Matthew 15:8) and making the Word of God of no effect through my religion or tradition.

> ***...making the word of God of no effect***
> ***through your tradition which you have***
> ***handed down. And many such things you do.***
> ***- Mark 7:13***

Regardless of your interpretation of the above verse, I recommend you ask yourself, am I allowing tradition, experience, and human reasoning to stop God's Word from even being given a chance to have an effect in my life?

Have you ever laid hands on the sick and not seen them recover (Mark 16:17-19)? I would say this is true of a lot of us. Does that mean God's Word is not to be believed? Maybe Mark 16 is supposed to say, "the anointed will lay hands", or perhaps "the pastor", or "the gifted," or some other man-made way that seems right, not "Believers?" Maybe, if you go to Bible College and spend the next 25 years of your life building tradition, Mark 16 will come true, right? Now do you refrain from laying hands because the reasoning of your experience says, "That doesn't work?" Do you now believe what God says or what man says (your experience)?

> *Maybe Mark 16 is supposed to say, "the anointed will lay hands"*

One of the things I discovered after hospital was that the Word says to lay hands, **believing**. I chose to start laying hands, believing "Your Word is true," not "I've had the right experiences", or "my feelings want me to", or "I mentally agree," and my experience (fruit) started to change. People began being healed. Don't try to make your experience matter more than believing God's Word. Don't let your experience make the Word of God of no effect and stop you from laying hands. I believe God's Word more than my experience, your experience, or anyone else's experience, and so should you.

A couple of ways that strongholds are created and strengthened in our lives are...

Songs

The impact of songs is incredible. I sincerely apologise to all the people I ever led in songs of bad doctrine. They are designed to be catchy and usually repetitive. We often forget the message of a sermon and leave a service singing these songs, and they're frequently on the radio in our cars on the way home. A danger of songs is that they demand our wilful participation. They require us to hear them (ears), read them (eyes), say them (mouth), and often emotion (soul) is attached to them. Song lyrics can be really dangerous. What are you singing religiously, deceiving your heart, believing because you repeat them? Truth?

Pastors

Pastors are people! They will tell you what they believe God is saying, but is it actually what God is saying or just someone's reasoning? One of the most dangerous things about pastors, like any profession, is that people value what they say and think what they are saying are the oracles of God, but are they? Do we elevate pastors into a position above God's Word?

Prayers

Not something to discuss lightly. Your prayer is between you and God, but are you declaring truth or just speaking what's on your mind? You can pray yourself into believing the wrong thing; alternatively, you can declare God's Word until you believe that.

I repeat communion because I believe in remembering Christ's sacrifice, discerning the Lord's body, and proclaiming His death and resurrection until He comes. This is repeating what I believe, and this is a religious activity I am for.

> *There is a vast difference between repeating what you believe and believing what you repeat.*

What are you doing religiously that contradicts what you believe and think that it has no cost? God says, *"He will never leave you nor forsake you"* (Hebrews 13:5), but in church, do you sing, "...take not Thy Holy Spirit from me," and pray for God to be with you? Do you believe He might leave you? We sing about a God who could part the waters again if He wanted to when it is clear that God told Moses to do it (Exodus 14:16), and a man with a word from God parted the sea. We pray and ask God to move the mountain when He told us to speak to the mountain (Mark 11:23).

> ***And the LORD said to Moses, "Why do you cry to Me? Tell the children of Israel to go forward. But lift up your rod, and stretch out your hand over the sea and divide it. And the children of Israel shall go on dry ground through the midst of the sea." - Exodus 14:15-16***

What's the solution, then? It depends on how quickly you want to renew your mind and walk and act in truth, but I would recommend a ruthless disregarding of anything that disagrees with the Word of God. Be it sermons, songs, false or negative confessions in prayer, books, feelings, and so on. Turn to faith in God and believe His Word, not just for the things we can't control but also for things we think we can. Taste and see.

~TESTIMONY~

One day, I asked God for more power in my words. He responded in question, as He often does, by asking me, "Do you want power in everything you say?" Wow! There were some things I was saying that I didn't want to have power. Imagine this... you want to say, "be healed," and see someone healed. Then you say to someone who just cut you off on the road, "I hope you crash!" Which words do you want there to be power in? Other examples are people who say they are dying to get somewhere, sick and tired of something, or things that make them mad.

Do you think God should decide which words have power and you are not responsible? Don't kid yourself! Fresh water and salt water don't come from the same well (James 3:11). The Bible tells you to take every thought captive (2 Corinthians 10:5) and that the tongue can turn your whole body (James 3:2). Don't think you can get away with religious repetition that is not the truth. Like a rudder turning a ship, your tongue changes the course that you're on. You cannot repeat what you don't believe and expect it to have no consequence. Do you want to see more fruit from your lips? Death and life are in the power of the tongue (Proverbs 18:21). Speak truth. Speak what you believe. Bless and do not curse (Romans 12:14).

> *Do you think God should decide which words have power?*

> ***Out of the same mouth proceed blessing
> and cursing. My brethren, these things
> ought not to be so. Does a spring send forth
> fresh water and bitter from the same
> opening? Can a fig tree, my brethren, bear
> olives, or a grapevine bear figs? Thus, no
> spring yields both salt water and fresh.***
> ***- James 3:10-12***

Since hospital, I have been choosing to speak the words that I believe Jesus would say if He were standing there in His flesh, believing that He *is* there standing in mine. I choose to believe His Word and step out in faith, because God's Word says I can (and so can you!). The result: people are being healed.

~BUILDING UP~

I'm going to say here what you probably already know. You need a **personal** relationship with Jesus; like building any relationship, **you** must be involved. Who is Jesus to you? Is He more than just a way to avoid hell? Are you willing to do life *with* Him, or do you think you can just thank Him for His sacrifice as you pass by Him on the way to Heaven? Relationship with Him is **by far** the most important thing in your life. Jesus died on the cross because He **desires** to do life with you, not because He so wanted you in heaven. If you stopped attending church, would your life still show that He is most important to you?

I'm not encouraging you to leave your place of worship but to ponder how different your life might look if you did. What if you could no longer rely on your pastor to tell you what they thought the Word of God said? How would your prayer life look if you were required to pray and not just say amen? How would you worship if you didn't have a team to follow? If you took communion at home, how would that look? What if you personally had to seek Jesus to be the author and perfecter of your faith (Hebrews 12:2)? I am an advocate for meeting together (Hebrews 10:25), but what I am saying is, how different would the service look if you had a group of people who came to express their **own** relationship with God and not just coming to agree with someone else's? People tell others they need a personal relationship with Jesus; religion is not that.

I am now personally choosing to acknowledge that God is with me every moment of every day. This motivates me to talk to Him without ceasing (1 Thessalonians 5:17), like a phone call from which I don't hang up. Now, I set time aside to give Him worship, praise Him, and thank Him for all He has done; for meeting my needs and leading me into all truth. Then I make time for Him to speak. When I worship Him, it's an overflow of my heart, not just singing words while trying to get my emotions in line with whatever is being said. I choose to read my Bible now and seek out what God is saying through it. I share with others what I think God is saying, to see if that's how they understand it and how they know Him, as I have no interest in believing a lie.

The choice to have a personal relationship with God the Father, Son and Holy Spirit is the most important choice you can make, and accepting salvation by grace is just the start.

FIVE

WHAT DOES GOD SAY?

I don't care what man says!

~PULLING DOWN~

I will no longer try to reason and make up a way that seems right, something that comforts my feelings. I will press in to knowing God and let Him show me what **is** right.

> ***However, when He, the Spirit of truth, has come, He will guide you into all truth; for He will not speak on His own authority, but whatever He hears He will speak; and He will tell you things to come. - John 16:13***

It is so incredible to me just how far I had shifted in my believing away from believing what God said. Almost to the point where I could say I was following a new religion - a religion of niceness. I would say this is exactly the same as what most unsaved people believe, only they don't give up their Sunday mornings or pay tithes, and I imagine they don't feel so bad about sinning. I am not saying that I wasn't responsible for seeking God for myself, but I had immersed myself in religion for years, and no one knew to or had been willing to, challenge my poor thinking or acting.

I think that the religion of niceness came about because people who knew God's Word tried to rewrite it in a way that explained their own or others' experiences. This is then repeated and passed on, and people like me start to believe man's word in place of God's. The Bible clearly tells us in Proverbs 3:5 not to lean on our own understanding, that the traditions of man could render God's Word useless (Mark 7:13). This tells me we should be hesitant (careful) to explain the Bible to others (James 3:1). As discussed in a later chapter, we start to minimise our living by faith, and we start to live by reasoning. I really want to get this point across: reason doesn't make you free; truth sets you free. I hope that from reading this book, you will see that I would discard my understanding if it were shown to be incorrect. I don't lean on it. Truth is much more desired than comfort. Do you agree?

> *We start to minimise our living by faith, and we start to live by reasoning.*

I now realise that my experiences were either aligned with the Word of God or were not the experiences I was supposed to have. I stopped looking at the Word through my experiences and started looking at my experiences through the Word. I realised that my understanding, or anyone else's, should not be leaned on, and it was wrong if it didn't agree with God's Word (Romans 3:4).

I quickly realised that translations and commentaries could be wrong. My favourite preachers could be wrong, regardless of how eloquent, persuasive or dynamic they were (1 Corinthians 2:1). When you make the choice that God's Word is true and that any interpretation could be wrong, including your own, suddenly,

> *I stopped looking at the Word through my experiences and started looking at my experiences through the Word.*

you start praying more intently that God would help you interpret the Word correctly (2 Timothy 2:15). Every word of every verse, the context, who it was written to, and what covenant they were in, etc. This all starts to matter. You must choose that the Word of God is true, even before you read it. Regardless of whether you understand it or your experience aligns with it - it is true.

Your experience never has and never will determine what the truth or the will of God is. Choose to accept it **as it is written**, not "as it is experienced." Choose to believe the Word, not false religion.

I recently watched a snippet of a popular TV show that gives a relatable reason for Jesus not healing someone. Weird, my Bible says that **ALL** who *came* to Him got healed. **ALL!** I would be lying to make up a reason for my failure to minister healing or your failure to receive healing. There are no reasons in the Bible for someone not being healed by Jesus. Unbelief and wrong belief has affected other people, but they are not my example. I would rather say truthfully, "I don't know." God's Word is truth.

The Word of God is true, even before you read it.

Make His words - your words. The Word describes who God is, who He is to me, and how my life should look, not religion. Not man's reasoning of their experience.

God gave me a picture and a question - if Jesus walked over to me reading the Word, pointed at a verse and said, "this is true", would I believe it more? I shouldn't believe it any more than I already do, but it sure would stir my faith to act on it.

In most cases, the Bible becomes surprisingly simple when you stop trying to make it say things to match your experiences and accept it **as it is written**. People talk about how the Bible tells you the truth you need to hear when you need to hear it. While Holy Spirit might highlight what's important to your present circumstance and say what you need to hear, the Bible is not rewriting itself to get you through something. God's Word will still say the same thing 5, 10, 50 or 1000 years from now. It is not going to change. We may grow in our understanding of it, as in, it gets clearer, but if you think it's different, then your understanding is or was wrong.

> ***Forever, O LORD,***
> ***Your word is settled in heaven.***
> ***Psalms 119:89***

~TESTIMONY~

When I came out of the hospital, I chose only to believe God's Word. That meant massive changes in what I believe and how I live. At the most foundational level, I knew I needed to reconsider which translation of the Bible I was reading. Words began to matter so much more. It started with looking in the Scripture for life but developed into a passion for His Word. I started praying so much more that I would hear what God was saying, not what a translator thought was the best English word out of a list of possibilities to use for a given Greek or Hebrew word. The difference between eternal life (aiōnios zōē - John 3:16) and saved (sōzō - John 3:17) started to matter much more. I brought friends around me that I knew cared more for the truth than my feelings, and I knew they cared enough to tell me if I believed wrongly, a way that seemed right to a man. I started guarding my heart and taking my thoughts captive, discerning what preaching, songs, and books I allow to speak into my life.

The result? I had peace. No longer was I tossed to and fro, because God's Word doesn't change. I was freer than I had ever been because I wasn't listening to people to find out whether what they said seemed right; I was listening to see if what they were saying was the same as what God said through His Word. If He said it, I believe it! I believe that just changed someone's heart as they read that!

~BUILDING UP~

If you are going to make any change in this area, you will need to make a very important decision.

I **will** believe God's Word above all else.

If you don't do this, you **will** make yourself like a wave tossed to and fro by any doctrine (Ephesians 4:14), any experience, feeling, song, book, preacher, and religious fad.

No longer should you look for ways the Bible might be applied to your experience. You will now look at your experience and see what the Bible says, what His will says, and have faith and perseverance to make your experience change to align with that. Make your experience change, don't twist the Scripture.

> *Make your experience change, don't twist the Scripture.*

I used to be proud of having a certain Bible translation because it was the 'thing' to have. Now, it is more important for me to know what God says regardless of the translation. This means that I pray and ask God to show me what He said. I read the Bible with the mindset of finding out what God is saying, what He wants me to hear, not just accepting what translators used as their word of choice. I am not trying to sound clever, harsh or judgmental here. Just look at the word "patience" in Galatians 5:22 and compare it with the word translated "patience" in James 1:3. They clearly have different meanings, but you only get one English word. Different translations put different words in these verses, and you need to know what God wanted you to hear.

I don't want to talk about healing too much here, but of the people I have ministered to recently, their healing came the second, third or seventh time I prayed. The point I want to get across here is that God said in Mark 16:17-18, that Believers will/shall/do lay hands on the sick, and they will/shall/do recover. I believe this the first time I pray, and I still believe it the seventh time. I choose to persevere because His Word is true. I accept His Word as truth and admit that any failure to minister or receive His promise is not something written in His Word. His Word is a solid rock, a firm foundation, forever settled, unchanging. I can choose to persevere and press in, or I can rewrite this verse to have an out clause like "sin", "generational curses", or a "Paul's thorn" to match any of my circumstances.

SIX

WHO IS IN CONTROL?

God paid a huge price for you to be able to choose, don't reject it!

~PULLING DOWN~

Before we start down this road, why does it seem like I have to convince the majority of people that bad stuff happening is **not** God's will? Some people are very creative and even seem intent on finding ways to call bad His will. Like a "Paul's thorn," "going through a Job experience," or "a blessing in disguise." People tend to call anything out of their control an "act of God." Shouldn't we be very hesitant to call anything bad, His will and look for ways that it isn't?

I suggest that there are two main reasons people do this. One is that people think saying that something happening apart from God's will is somehow saying that God is less powerful. Is that what they are saying when they sin? Did God become less powerful when Adam ate from the wrong tree? Two, if you can't call something bad God's will, it leaves us pondering the weight of our responsibility. Can we affect what happens?

I hope the next two chapters will address this clearly and encourage you to, as James 4:7 says, submit to what is His will and resist what isn't.

Jesus Christ on the cross is proof that man made something happen that God didn't will.

> ***...for all have sinned and fall short of the
> glory of God, - Romans 3:23***

Isn't that interesting? This verse literally says that every single person has made something happen that God didn't will!

> ***But God demonstrates His own love toward
> us, in that while we were still sinners,
> Christ died for us.
> - Romans 5:8***

I don't know that I can call all of heaven and earth to be witnesses like God did in Deuteronomy 30:19, but He said that we can bless and we can curse. That says that you and I have, at the very least, the ability to influence how the future goes. If you won't believe Him, you are not likely to believe me.

Is God in control? Many songs, sermons, books, and movies seem to think so. Are they right? Does the Bible agree? What do you think this means if you say it? To have any meaningful conversation about this, we need to define what is meant by "God is in control."

By saying that God is in control, I understand that to mean God is causing or allowing everything to happen. Everything happens for a reason, and that reason is because God willed it and chose for it to happen. Is that how you understand it? This is how I used to think.

I now say, "God is Sovereign." I am saying that God can do anything and is answerable to no-one. He is all-powerful, has all authority, outside of time, etc., but is bound by His own words,

> *Even the demons believe God could do anything, and tremble.*

which He cannot break (Hebrews 6:18). What He says, and what He said, goes! It is forever settled (Psalm 119:89). He magnified His Word above His name (Psalm 138:2).

If you believe God is in control, you accept your future. The most you can have faith for is to receive salvation and believe that He is still good despite attributing works of the devil to Him. Even the demons believe God could do anything and tremble.

In my opinion, this is the biggest false religious stronghold there is. God paid a huge price, sending His Son to die for your choices, not for His. You may say we are saying the same thing here, but there is a big difference in how we believe and act. The term itself should be offensive to you. Saying "God is in control" means that everything is going the way He wants, and praying His will be done is pointless. The term "God is sovereign" means that things aren't necessarily going the way He wants, and all things are possible to Him who believes, especially when we pray His will **be** done.

> *Therefore, do not be unwise,*
> *but understand what the will*
> *of the Lord is. - Ephesians 5:17*

People who say that God is in control, seem to pray, "Your will, whatever that is, be done." Ephesians 5:17 tells us to know His will. This verse means nothing if there are no wills other than His that can be known. We are told to pray His will **be** done in Matthew 6:10. There is no reason for praying this if His will is going to happen anyway. There is no purpose to praying "not my will," if it's only His will that eventuates.

Is there another option? Either God makes everything happen, or there are other wills at play.

I have heard of some envelope theory where you are only allowed to do bad to some degree so that, somehow, you can still say God is in control. These people would have to admit that all of the suffering in the world and in history is, or was within, someone's envelope. They just don't like to think they are capable of it. We need to understand that God has given us unrestricted ability to choose good (life) or bad (death). Become someone who, like Christ, lays down your will to do your Father's.

To find out where you stand currently, ask yourself the following questions:

- Can I sin?

- Does God let me sin (set before me death), or make me sin?

- If He lets someone else sin and it hurts me, is God responsible, or the person who sinned responsible?

- If only what God wants to happen occurs, how are **all** things possible to him who believes?

- If everything is going the way God wants it, what am I supposed to resist?

- If everything is happening the way God wants it to, why does He need to work to make it good for me?

- Am I as close to God as He wants or as I want? Read that one again.

- If God's will always happens, why do we pray His will be done?

You could ask many questions here, but I can't see how any of these allow you to say, "God is in control." Do you believe that saying, "God is in control," is a truthful thing to say? Define for yourself what "control" means and ask that question again.

Is God a Liar? NO!

Is God a liar? No! Did God sovereignly set before you life and death, blessing and cursing? Yes. If God set death before you, and you tried to choose it, would He be breaking His Word to take it back? Yes. Therefore, you have control of at least that choice. Is God less powerful because He gave us the ability to choose? No. He chose what words to say but cannot choose which words to keep.

Romans 8:28 shows us that God can masterfully work things for good. Not leave things alone because they're already going the way He wants, and not leave things alone and hope for the best. God gives us directions (Isaiah 30:21); this is unnecessary if you are already going the way He wants. He provides a way out when we are tempted (1 Corinthians 10:13). Don't dare say that God is tempting you. If God is not tempting you, does that not tell you other wills are happening?

Let no one say when he is tempted, "I am tempted by God;" for God cannot be tempted by evil, nor does He Himself tempt anyone. - James 1:13

Wherever you find a "might" in the Bible, there is a might not. John 3:17 says that all "might" be saved. John 10:10 says that you "might" have life. Ephesians 2:10 says that there are works that we "should" or "might" walk in them. Who chooses if you walk in them? Eternal life is not a "might." Romans 10:9 says that you **will** be saved. You either have it or you don't. John 3:16 does not say "might", but John 3:17 does - know the difference. Saved (sōzō) is something you "might" have on earth, but it's not just inherited because you have eternal life.

When God says in Luke 10:19 that He has given you authority over every work of the enemy, do you think that if nothing changes the first time you resist, it was God's will, and He will work out what happens from there? Do you imagine that God was just saying, "Have a go," or was He saying, "Get my will accomplished?" There's a huge difference in whether you think you're responsible for accomplishing God's will on earth or not. Your belief of whether God is in control **greatly** affects your choice to, and how you, resist. I talk about resisting separately in a later chapter.

I found this an interesting thing to do. Following a suggestion, I searched for the word "sovereign" in the KJV Bible. I got zero results. Then I did the same search in the NIV. I got 304. Imagine what the wrong definition of sovereign, like "God is in control", could do. Now in reading your Bible, you may be hearing the wrong thing, not a couple of times, but over 300 times. You need to know what you're supposed to be hearing. What is truth?

His will is not always done.

Firstly, we need to accept that wills other than His exist and happen. Just because something is happening doesn't mean it is God's will that it does. Second, we need to accept that His will is not always done. 1 Timothy 2:4 says that it is God's will that **all** be saved. Do all accept Jesus' sacrifice?

Here is a story I believe God showed me to help understand control…

If I sit down to watch TV with my son and say, "We're going to watch what I decide," I'm in control. But if I give the remote to my son and say, "We'll watch whatever you decide," life or death, he has the choice. He can choose to watch something good or not. I'd be breaking my word to take the remote back and stop him from watching something I didn't like. No one doubts that I have the power to take the remote back, but I'd have to go back on my word if I did. Just because I WON'T go back on my word (Psalms 138:2, Psalm 119:89, Psalm 15:4) doesn't mean there's nothing I can do. This is where Romans 8:28 and 1 Corinthians 10:13 start being applied. I could get the family around and have my son's favourite food, offering him some. I could offer to get his best mate to join us for some gaming. I could do a lot of things that would make it easier for him to make a different choice, but the choice is his. I want my children to know that I care for them and want the best for them. I say, "This is the way; choose life." I want them to make choices that are loving to me or others, but ultimately, the fruit of the spirit is **self**-control. I choose my words very carefully because I don't want to break my word and take them back.

If you still believe God is in control, you can't believe in a better future (faith), and you can't resist in the present. Everything becomes something He's doing, so you just ask God for wisdom to understand it. A ridiculous number of songs repeat this theme, and again I say, it is possibly the biggest stronghold you will ever pull down, but it allows you to believe God's Word. I discovered how different the Bible reads when you come to this understanding and accept it.

Speak the truth, don't call God a liar. He is sovereign, omnipotent, and omnipresent, but is not controlling everything.

~TESTIMONY~

While in hospital, all I knew to believe was that I was in there because God needed it; it was all part of His master plan. I was even asked by a friend I greatly respect, "Why do you think you're in here?" Being as holy as I was (just kidding), I said it must've been for someone else. This is when I listened to the song with the lyrics, "What would you do if He walked into the room?" I realised in that moment that so much of what I had believed didn't even make sense if He, Jesus, walked into that room. I knew in a heart-beat that what I had believed was wrong. This set me on a new journey of pursuing truth. The most foundational truth was I was not unwell because God willed it. If God didn't will it, it was time to find out what He did will and pray **it** be done.

God is not mocked. You reap what you sow. I realised that if I wanted someone to come heal me, even if it were Christ Himself, it was time for me to start ministering healing myself. Do unto others! The results have been exceedingly, abundantly more than I could have imagined. Since hospital, I went from hardly ever ministering healing to seeing it happen regularly. I was immediately faced with people giving me strange doctrines, trying to reason my success, like God giving special anointing to those battling illness. What? Where is that in the Bible? The truth is, those who need healing find out that it's God's will and then start believing

> *"…or you just get healed."*

His Word. Lay hands believing! You can do that without being sick.

One of the most memorable healings I've been a part of ministering so far, was a friend who was in hospital with a perforated bowel. He messaged me and said that he was told he had to go on a liquid diet with strong antibiotics and if that didn't work, have surgery to fix part of his bowel. I remember feeling bold when I messaged him back, saying, "...or you just get healed." Shortly after, another of our mutual friends invited me to go and pray for him in person. I remember feeling tired and wanting to stay home and watch TV, but I chose to ignore my feelings and go. There is more to the story, but we got to the hospital and prayed for him. Just after we left, they took blood tests, which had to be carried out twice, as the first one showed the bacterial count had dropped so much that they had to double-check it. Within 2-3 days, he was out of hospital and was eating fast-food by the weekend. The doctors said they were surprised at how quickly he had recovered. To my knowledge, he hasn't had an issue since.

The key point is that people are unwell for a will other than God's, and who knows what would happen if you went and prayed. You know what happens if you don't.

~BUILDING UP~

So, what does it mean if I choose to believe that God is "sovereign" and not "in control?"

The first thing that happened for me when I corrected my belief in this area, was that my love for God greatly increased. The God I knew was now so much more amazing. When He says, "love others as I have loved you", now I had a clearer understanding of what that meant. Being loving got immediately and incredibly more pure. I was no longer trying to reason why a good and loving God would do or allow bad stuff. The Bible started making so much more sense.

No longer saying God is in control means you are admitting that there are things that happen that are His will, things that happen that are not, and things He wanted to happen that didn't. There is a God to whom we submit, and there is a devil to resist (James 4:7). This, for me, was a **life-altering** realisation because now I had to know what His will was if I was going to have faith for it **to** happen. It meant there was a war I needed to fight. Therefore, I needed to put my armour on to be ready for battle. I was now aware of my responsibility to, as 1 Timothy 6:12 says, fight the good fight. Now I knew why I had to believe and live in a way that saves myself and others. No longer was I singing that I believe God could if He wanted to, and then waiting until His plan played out. I sense that I just enlisted some soldiers here!

> *No longer was I singing that I believe God could if He wanted to.*

Your future can be changed by what you believe and have faith for. All things are now possible to you, not just the things that were part of God's "unknowable" plan. This is so very amazing! When Jesus says your faith can move a mountain, you don't need to make sure it's His will that the mountain moves before you have faith and believe you receive. Knowing that God wants the mountain moved will strengthen you to **persevere** in moving it, but now you can believe that you receive when you pray (Mark 11:24), not just when you do or don't get it.

Now you can **persevere** in what you believe for. God wants you to prevail against the gates of hell. God wants you to take back what the enemy stole. This may mean you come up against some gates of hell that will try to stop you, but we aren't supposed to see the gate and say God is in control, "it mustn't be His will." We are to bring the gate down and not let it prevail against the church.

It means that maybe the circumstances you find yourself in, weren't willed by our loving Father for you to have and should be resisted in faith. Some of you need to read that again.

One of the things that I had to get comfortable with, was saying, "I don't know." As Paul says, "I don't claim to apprehend." An example would be when believing for the healing of someone, I had nowhere to turn if I didn't see His will accomplished except to say, "I don't know"! I used to make up some excuse or lean on false religion as to how it was somehow God's will, and this failure to receive was somehow better. There is a big issue when people alter their perception of God to call evil good. Just because someone fails to receive something, i.e., salvation or healing, does not mean that Jesus failed to bear the stripes, die on the cross for them, and provide.

> *I used to make up some excuse or lean on false religion.*

When you pull down this stronghold, the enemy will show you your past and try to condemn you. The enemy will start to show you all the things that might have gone differently if you had understood your responsibility, position and authority in Christ to resist. You **need to** respond by thanking the Lord that you are no longer that person. You are forgiven and not condemned. As Paul encourages us to do - forget what is behind and press on. Ask Him for wisdom in how to move forward and grace (strength in weakness) to do it.

The question to ask yourself is, can I affect whether God's will happens or not? Yes!

> **Brethren, I do not count myself to
> have apprehended; but one thing I do,
> forgetting those things which are
> behind and reaching forward to those
> things which are ahead, I press toward the
> goal for the prize of the upward call of God
> in Christ Jesus.**
> **Philippians 3:13-14**

SEVEN

ALLOWED?

Isn't everything that happens allowed?

~PULLING DOWN~

Hopefully, from the previous chapter, you now agree with me that things happen that are not the will of God. But what happens when you pray, and the mountain doesn't move? A lot of people seem to conclude that God "allowed" it. Once again, people would rather challenge God's will than question if their living influenced the result.

Before we continue, if you think God allowed something, what does that mean to you? I would suggest that a lot of people define "allowed" as God chose "not to do" something. God didn't make the bad thing happen, but He didn't stop it. But isn't that the same as willing it to happen but with a new name, "allowed"; God choosing "for" it to happen, making it His will that it does? I feel that this would go around in circles. This definition of allowed is exactly the same thing as something happening according to God's will. Things happen that are not His will.

Things happen that are not His will.

Questions to ponder...

- When God gave Adam the choice to love Him, did He allow him not to?

- When God gave Adam the freedom to follow His voice, did He allow him not to?

- Did God allow Adam and Eve to eat from the wrong tree, when He told them not to?

- Did God allow them to sin and not obey His command?

- Did He allow death to enter the world through their sin?

- Did He allow you to choose to sin?

- Did He allow you to curse when He allowed you to bless?

- Did He allow you to choose death when He allowed you to choose life?

- Can you choose to love Him?

- Can you choose to obey His voice?

These things are not a result of God choosing "not to do" something but the result of God choosing "to do" something. He let Adam choose.

More questions to ponder…

- Did God pre-program Lucifer only to love Him for a little while and then to be jealous of the throne?

- Did God pre-program him to test Job?

- Did He pre-program him to tempt Jesus?

- Is God going to punish him in hell for a choice that he didn't get to make?

- Did God pre-program all of us?

- Will we be rewarded or punished for something we don't get to choose?

Deuteronomy 30:19 tells us that the largest possible witness has been called; that you can choose. If God gave you the freedom to choose life, did He allow you to choose death?

There is no verse I am aware of stating that Lucifer could or couldn't choose, so you will have to go on who you know God is. Here's my opinion. The God I know is just. That means that people or created beings are accountable for their choices. God is good and wills that none should perish. The Bible tells us that the unrighteous will perish (Revelation 20:15), and there are those who seem eager for that.

So, when did God choose "not to do" something? People seem to immediately think of Paul's thorn and Job. I want to look at both of these accounts and share some insight I gained from what the Bible says.

~PAUL'S THORN~

And lest I should be exalted above measure by the abundance of the revelations, a thorn in the flesh was given to me, a messenger of Satan to buffet me, lest I be exalted above measure. Concerning this thing I pleaded with the Lord three times that it might depart from me. And He said to me, "My grace is sufficient for you, for My strength is made perfect in weakness." Therefore, most

gladly I will rather boast in my infirmities, that the power of Christ may rest upon me. Therefore, I take pleasure in infirmities, in reproaches, in needs, in persecutions, in distresses, for Christ's sake. For when I am weak, then I am strong.

- 2 Corinthians 12:7-10

Why was this thorn given? Pride? A thorn was given to hinder God or His Word being revealed to and through Paul. People seem to view this record as God not wanting Paul to get into pride. Who was giving Paul His abundance of revelations? God! God was revealing Himself to Paul. If God wanted to, couldn't He have just stopped revealing Himself? Isn't God a rewarder of those who diligently seek Him? When we draw near to Him, doesn't He draw near to us? Isn't eternal life that we know Him? Doesn't He desire that all men come to a knowledge of the truth? If you start to know God abundantly, would God need to give you a thorn? It makes much more sense that the devil would want to "buffet" people knowing and revealing God. Do you think Paul was being proud when he said this…

To me, who am less than the least of all the saints, this grace was given, that I should preach among the Gentiles the unsearchable riches of Christ, Ephesians 3:8

What was given? What was this thorn? This verse clearly states that it was a messenger of Satan. A messenger of Satan was given to Paul, so why do people think it was sickness? Do they think Paul was telling a little white lie because he didn't want to say he was sick? If Paul didn't call it sickness, why do so many people?

Maybe you read the word infirmity as sickness and infer that is what it meant. Using the same reasoning, you could say that Paul's thorn was persecutions. People seem to call anything that doesn't change after a prayer or two, a "Paul's thorn." What makes something the will of God? Experience, or His word?

On a side note, infirmity can mean sickness, or it can just mean I have just been stoned, shipwrecked, beaten with rods, and it is hard to hold a pen and write to you. If sickness was never mentioned in the list of all Paul's trials, why do people re-write their bible to add that in?

Who gave this messenger, God or Satan? If you take the Bible **as it is written**, it clearly states a messenger of Satan. People tend to believe this record reads "God-given." Don't be deceived. Just because something happens doesn't mean it is God. When you read this now, is it not clear to you that the devil assigned a messenger to make Paul's life hard?

This account shows us that a being, a messenger of satan, who God had "allowed" to rebel against Him when created, was. Could God have broken His word and just stopped this being from rebelling? Do you think God can set death before you and then take the choice back when He wants? Kind of makes our choice to love Him seem worthless if that's our only choice.

I am not making up scripture here, just offering my thoughts, but why was Paul talking to *God* about resisting this messenger and not just resisting it himself? Like Moses pleading with God, and God saying why are you crying out to me? I have heard it said, don't ask God to do anything He has told you to do, and He said to resist the devil. This passage does not mention that Paul resisted this messenger himself, but rather that He asked God to, and God obviously did not. People read this as "allowed", but maybe God just didn't want to break His Word.

> *Everything you will face in your life, is something that God allowed.*

As you begin to see that not all things are God's will or "allowed," you start asking what is your responsibility as an ambassador of Christ, a representative of God's Kingdom? You resist harder and persevere (stand) longer. In Mark 9:19, when the disciples failed to heal the boy with the mute spirit, Jesus did not say, this is a thorn and won't come out. Jesus got it done. Don't call your unwillingness to persevere, a thorn. If the disciples were still resisting when Jesus showed up, do you think he would have berated them? Not likely.

The last point I want to make on this, is that God did not say He was choosing not to do something. He DID NOT SAY He was "allowing" it. He DID SAY, "My grace is sufficient." Everything you will face in your life is something that God has allowed, but His grace is sufficient. He hears you; He always hears you. You may have a mountain you're commanding to move, a sickness or a messenger of satan in your life. Keep declaring God's Word, standing, resisting, and giving place to grace. Let no weapon prosper, or gate prevail. You are more than a conqueror, you are an overcomer, and the Lord shall lead you in triumph and victory. Again, His grace is sufficient for you. Allow His strength to be made perfect in your weakness.

~JOB~

I had never really understood why we had the book of Job other than having an example of a man who suffered more than most of us and did it reasonably honourably. When writing this chapter, I believe God showed me two incredible points I hadn't seen before.

> ***So Satan answered the LORD and said, "Does Job fear God for nothing? Have You not made a hedge around him, around his household, and around all that he has on every side? You have blessed the work of his hands, and his possessions have increased in the land. But now, stretch out Your hand and touch all that he has, and he will surely curse You to Your face!" And the LORD said to Satan, "Behold, all that he has is in your power; only do not lay a hand on his person." So Satan went out from the presence of the LORD. - Job 1:9-12***

Firstly, Job, his wife, and his friends believed that God was in control. That everything happening to him was somehow God. He didn't know better. This seems to be the case with most Christians I talk to. This account clearly shows us who was responsible for bringing the strife, NOT God, but the devil. What happens when you think God is doing everything? You submit to it, get frustrated, angry, confused, feel helpless and defeated, unable to have faith that your circumstances change. You start changing your view of God to include every evil thing. You have the book of Job. You know better.

Secondly, the Devil, unresisted, will steal, kill and destroy. I pray that you will get this point. God did not "allow" the devil to do anything he wasn't already "allowed" to do. He didn't make him more evil all of a sudden. He, however, did choose to stop resisting him, the very thing He commands us to do. God showed us what happens when the devil is not resisted. Once again, most Christians I talk to don't resist the devil. They ask God to and seem confused when His response is, "My grace is sufficient." I don't pretend to understand why God decided to resist less on Job's behalf; God is God, after all. I don't claim to have apprehended, but I do know that God repeatedly tells us in the New Testament to resist the devil. This DOES NOT mean that you ask God to do it; it means that you can live in a way where the devil flees from you.

> *The devil, unresisted, will steal, kill and destroy.*

Behold, I give you the authority to trample on serpents and scorpions, and over all the power of the enemy, and nothing shall by any means hurt you. - Luke 10:19

When God says "all" in the above verse, this means we can resist as much for ourselves as God did for Job. God tells us to resist. Will you? You have been given authority. This verse DOES NOT say, "Behold, I give you permission to ask Me." Jesus gives the example of how to resist the devil, in His name, with the blood and the word of your testimony, with truth, as it is written, with a word, be loosed, declare what you want to happen, overcome evil with good.

The best understanding I can offer on 'allowing', is that it is the degree to which the devil is resisted. How much is he resisted in your life? What do *you* allow?

The last thing I would like to discuss in my attempt to destroy this stronghold is whether God allows bad things to occur to make a prophecy happen. Everything that happens is allowed. We believe in a God who transcends time, who knows the end from the beginning, and then prophesies that through people. The question people have is, does God have to "do" anything to make the future go the way He told us it will go?

> **Then the eyes of the blind**
> **shall be opened,**
> **And the ears of the deaf**
> **shall be unstopped. - Isaiah 35:5**

For this to happen, did God have to cause blindness?

> **Now as Jesus passed by, He saw a man who**
> **was blind from birth. And His disciples**
> **asked Him, saying, "Rabbi, who sinned, this**

*man or his parents, that he was born
blind?" Jesus answered, "Neither this man
nor his parents sinned, but that the works
of God should be revealed in him."
- John 9:1-3*

It's one thing to see and reveal things of the future, and it's another thing entirely to cause the future to happen the way you want. The latter doesn't even need you to see the future; you can just do what you say you will. Imagine a firefighter who wants to be seen putting out fires, so he lights one to be seen fighting. God didn't make things happen for Jesus to fix. He saw Jesus' future, and revealed through prophets what His life would do.

~BUILDING UP~

Was it God's will to test Job? No! It was the desire of Satan. Was Paul's thorn something God willed? No! It was the desire of Satan. Is something happening to you that is the desire of Satan and not the will of God? Just because it's happening does not make it God's will. We can be very sure of one thing: if the devil gets his way, he will devour you. The devil needed God to remove His hedge of protection in order to touch Job. He needed

God to stop resisting him; God has now given us the authority and responsibility to resist.

First of all, fear God (Proverbs 1:7). Satan wants to sift you (Luke 22:31). It's his desire; he wants to steal, kill and destroy you (John 10:10). He is roaming about seeking whom he may devour (1 Peter 5:8). Don't give him a foothold. Dwell in the shadow of the Most High (Psalms 91:1-6). People love to ask God for protection when we could live a life that is protected. People seem to think that if they ask God nicely, His shadow will move over them. This is not what the scripture says. We can choose to move or stay under His shadow. Ask Him for wisdom in what to believe and how to live.

Jesus hopes that we **might** inherit the blessing of Abraham (Galatians 3:14). What are those blessings? Read Deuteronomy 28. You should see some similarities to what Job had. Jesus hopes that we **might** get them. He desires

> *What excuse would Jesus give to "allow" someone to continue in sickness?*

that all men **might** be sōzō. If something is hindering you from receiving sōzō, walking in the blessing of Abraham, it probably isn't God. If something is stealing, killing or destroying, resist first and ask questions later. I'd rather get to heaven and have God tell me I was resisting Him by accident, than be told I let some bad things happen because I didn't resist.

The question I had to wrestle with, was what excuse would Jesus give to "allow" someone to continue in sickness if He walked in the room and someone came to Him for healing? There is no such example given. He wouldn't! So why do people come up with one? Better to stand in faith on His Word than to come up with some understanding and lean on that.

EIGHT

KNOW HIS WILL

*Understand what
the will of the Lord is*

~PULLING DOWN~

When you pray, "His will be done," are you praying for the accomplishment of something unknowable, or are you speaking what God's will **is** and having faith for it to occur? Are you aware that you influence whether His will happens or not? Do you believe you have received it **when** you pray? It's rather hard to believe you have received something when you add, "*if* it be Thy will."

> ***Therefore, I say to you, whatever things you ask when you pray, believe that you receive them, and you will have them. - Mark 11:24***

I think that probably the most definitive verse in the Bible to show us that God is not causing everything to happen, that there are wills besides His, is Ephesians

5:17. It tells us to **know** His will. For what reason should we know His will? So that we can have faith for it to occur, submit our will to it, and resist what we know isn't His will. He tells us to know His will, which means it **is** knowable. There are "facts" you are unlikely to know, like the intricate details of how babies form in the womb, but you should know His will that you are to clothe the naked. You should never need to ask Him what His will is on something if you have already been told in His Word.

> *What does God say to the saved?*

A key reason people struggle in this area is because of a rather frustrating deception that God's ways are higher than our ways (Isaiah 55:8). Please take a moment to settle this. Read verse 7 and ask yourself, who is He talking to. He is talking to the wicked and the unrighteous. Is this still how you identify? If you are saved, you are no longer unrighteous and wicked; you need to ask yourself, what does He say to the saved? **Understand** what the will of the Lord is. Stop saying we can't know His will. Find it out! Read this verse - we have the mind of Christ (1 Corinthians 2:16), and this one - for a servant does not know what his master is doing, but I have called you friends (John 15:5). Don't take my word for it, look these verses up yourself and settle the matter It is not only possible to know His will, but it is supposed to be known.

Let the wicked forsake his way,
And the unrighteous man his thoughts;
Let him return to the LORD,
And He will have mercy on him;
And to our God,
For He will abundantly pardon.
"For My thoughts are not your thoughts,
Nor are your ways My ways,"
says the LORD.
Isaiah 55:7-8

The Bible contains many instances where God tells us what His will is. Will you ignore it, let your experiences try and dictate it, and ask Him to repeat Himself because you don't think you're supposed to know? Will you ask our Father, "Should I give this thirsty person a drink, in case it's not Your will?"

~TESTIMONY~

When I realised that I actually had say so in whether His will got done on earth, that it wasn't just done automatically, I started choosing to do the things that I **knew** were His will. I started blessing people because now I knew it made a difference. I started being careful with my words because I didn't want to curse myself or others. I said what I believed God would say. I chose to dwell in Him on purpose, not giving place to anxious thought or making room for my heart to be troubled.

I started doing the things I would want done to and for me. I started visiting the sick, intending to see them healed, share the gospel and blessing them with goods in their trial. When you understand that He doesn't just make you do His will when it suits, you start doing His will even when it doesn't suit. I don't need to have the right feelings to obey and do what I believe is His will.

...start doing His will even when it doesn't suit.

~BUILDING UP~

Here are some verses where He tells us His will,

- love God - Matthew 22:37

- love people - Matthew 22:39

- that you would seek first the kingdom and His righteousness - Mathew 6:33

- that you would forgive - Ephesians 4:32

- that all men be saved (sōzō) - 1 Timothy 2:4

- that you might be saved (sōzō)- John 3:17

- that you might have life - John 10:10

- that you might receive the Holy Spirit - Acts 2:38

- that you might inherit the blessing of Abraham - Galatians 3:14

- that you would rejoice always - 1 Thessalonians 5:16

- that you would pray continually - 1 Thessalonians 5:17

- that you would visit the widow and the orphan - James 1:27

- that you would come to a knowledge of the truth - 1 Timothy 2:4

- that you would prosper and be in health - 3 John 1:2

- that you would preach the gospel and heal the sick - Matthew 10:7-8

- that you would speak in tongues and prophesy - 1 Corinthians 14:5

- that you would submit to God and resist the devil - James 4 :7

- that you would consider the testing of your faith pure joy - James 1:2-3

- that you would make disciples - Matthew 28:19

- that you would be humble - 1 Peter 5:6

- that you would be strong and courageous - Joshua 1:9

- that you would walk in the plans He has for you - Jeremiah 29:11 and Ephesians 2:10   ... and on and on.

who desires all men to be saved and to come to the knowledge of the truth.
1 Timothy 2:4

Know *His will and pray that! Let me say that again! Pray that the will that is* **known** *be done.*

NINE

HIS WAY OR YOUR WAY

He says go, but are you too busy singing "God send revival" to move?

~PULLING DOWN~

**He who dwells in the secret place
of the Most High
Shall abide under the shadow
of the Almighty. - Psalms 91:1**

Notice this verse does not say "he whom His shadow covers." Imagine it's raining, and there's nowhere to take shelter. Then you see God is holding out an umbrella, but instead of going and standing under it, you stand in the rain, praying that God will move the umbrella to you. People seem to prefer asking God to bless their way instead of doing things His way, which is already blessed.

God says, *"I will keep in perfect peace those whose minds are stayed on Him"* (Isaiah 26:3). People choose not to keep their minds stayed on Him; they spend their time watching TV and scrolling social media, etc., and pray for and expect peace. Do you want peace? God has told you His way. Why not do that?

Are you doing things the way that was reasoned by man and not what was instructed by God? What if that reasoning was making the Word of God of no effect? The promises of God are inherited by faith and persevering, not coming up with your own way.

> ***...that you do not become sluggish, but imitate those who through faith and patience inherit the promises.***
> ***Hebrews 6:12***

When the disciples said in Mark 9:28, "Why could we not cast it out?" Jesus did not say, "because you can't" or "because you are doing it wrong." He told them what to do about unbelief in their lives. He didn't give them a new method to try that might have more success but instructed them on what they needed in their life. Prayer: intentional connection with the Father. Fasting: intentional *dis*connection with the world. Not "a" prayer, not "a" fast, but prayer and fasting, relationship, lifestyle. We may face promises of

Jesus didn't give them a new method.

God that are harder to receive, but God's Word doesn't change to suit; it's forever settled (Psalms 119:89). If we fail to inherit a promise of God doing what He says, we need to be willing to say "I don't know," Your Word is true! Pray, "God, I need wisdom." Don't come up with your own methods and reasoning, making the Word of God of null effect.

Religious thinking can get you doing things a new way, thinking that you are pleasing the Father when you are just worshipping Him in vain (Mathew 15:9). An example of this is people who sing, "God send revival," denying God has put Himself in them and said **go** (Mathew 28:19). According to Colossians 1:27, Christ in you is the hope of revival happening, God being glorified on earth. Everywhere you go, revival should happen. God walks in you and talks in you. People experience God in you, and you bring the kingdom near to them. God did send revival - He sent you!

People appear to want God to do something they are not responsible for, like causing a revival meeting they can attend or controlling them like puppets instead of just choosing to obey what He said. They seem to think that God needs to do something else or more like He hasn't already done enough. God **has** done something! He sent His son, Jesus at the whipping post, Jesus on the Cross, His death, His resurrection, the sending of Holy

Spirit! He put Himself in you hoping that you would show His glory on the earth.

The signs and wonders performed by the apostles in Acts 2 were not God making people do things against their will. It was people who realised that God was with them, and they submitted to Him. They had flames of fire to show the presence of God was with them, the baptism of Holy Spirit. What do you need, to realise God is with you? Where do you find it in the Bible that you should only heal the sick and preach the gospel when you have a tongue of fire on your head?

Didn't people appear drunk? I personally believe God moved in a way that people were so aware of Him they didn't realise they were naked (Genesis 3:7). I don't want you to think that I am making this sign and wonder seem less miraculous. There are amazing moves of God, and this was one of them. I pray for them to happen! God wants us to be so filled with Him (Ephesians 5:18) that we are emptied of ourselves and may appear drunk to others. I think deep down, we desire for God to do something we can't control, that we may boast we had an encounter or were used by Him. Do you really think God makes people do things against their will? If you are submitted to Him, you will do His will even if this makes you look foolish. There is no mention of Adam and Eve being drunk, no mention of Jesus appearing drunk, or

Paul. I know that God could do exceedingly more than I think, put a tongue of fire on my head, make me so aware of Him I appear drunk, but I don't need this to obey His Word. I don't seek an experience, I seek Him!

Do you think God is teaching you a "new" way? There seems to be a large number of books, videos and blogs about how people believe God is teaching them a new way in their trial. He definitely teaches people when they draw near to Him in their trial, but God is not likely teaching us something new, rather showing us what we should already have known.

> *Do you think God is teaching you a "new" way?*

There are many ways people try to get a manifestation of God. I have experienced the change first-hand when you make Him more a part of your life, and then do things His way. His way is true. His way works. His way is the way. He is the way. People want to make Him 2% of their lives and expect 110% of His power to flow, and if that doesn't work, they try a new way.

When has someone been called a good teacher when their student doesn't know what they should be learning? How often do people say that God is teaching them something through their suffering but have no idea what? He is the **good** Teacher! If He were teaching you something that wasn't already in the textbook, the Bible, I'd be rather surprised. Do you think God wants to teach you something that He doesn't want everyone to learn? Does everyone need to go through their own trial to learn what you are learning? If you are suffering and don't know why, it's probably a good indication that you should be resisting, not asking for wisdom.

Don't call your failure to inherit a promise of God, Him teaching you something. We have the mind of Christ, and we have the Word. Holy Spirit is leading you into all truth, but are you saying you need this trial too? Really? Be careful not to call evil good. (Isaiah 5:20) Pressing in to God, praying and reading His Word is teaching me. Sickness has taught me nothing more than that I don't want to be sick. God has definitely

> *God, there's a sea in the way, can you part it for me?*

produced hupomonē (James 1:2-3, discussed in a later chapter) in my life through sickness, He has worked great things out of it, but He didn't cause it; I fell into it.

Speak to the mountain, not to God about the mountain. You are praying religiously if you ask God to move the mountain for you. He has told you to speak to it. This is the same religious thinking that says God parted the sea. A man with a word from God parted the sea. Do you have it in your head that Moses said to God, "God, there's a sea in the way; can you part it for me?" and God said, "Well, because you asked so nicely and skipped lunch today, I'll do something about that for you." NO! God said, "Why are you crying out to me, you part the sea" (Exodus 14:15-16), and Moses did.

~TESTIMONY~

A massive freedom I now have as a follower of Christ, is that if I know His will on something, I just do it. If I would want something done for myself, I do it for others. I don't wait to see if God wants me to move; He has already told me to go. Does God want to encourage people? Yes! Then that's what I do, and I ask the Holy Spirit to help me do it effectively. I don't know that I can express strongly enough the freedom of knowing what should be done and just doing it. I often pray that God would lead me to give love where it's most needed, but while I wait for any guidance, I'm loving the person in front of me.

I believe it's always His will to heal and that He has told me to do it, so I at least lay hands believing. I know it's always His will for people to be in peace, so I live peaceably and make peace as much as I can. I choose to be quick to listen and slow to speak, not because I feel like it, but because I know that's what He wants. I believe He is generous, and I want people to be generous with me, so I am generous with others. Jesus is the truth; the truth makes you free, and who the Son sets free is free indeed. I know I am more free than I have ever been.

~BUILDING UP~

We need to stop trying to find ways that seem right to a man. If we want Biblical results, we must do what the Bible instructs. We can no longer do things our way and ask God to bless that. We need to do things His way, the way that is already blessed. We need to become fully persuaded, steadfast in His Word, endure, persevere (hupomonē), and when we have done all, to stand (Ephesians 6:13), not try and make up a new way.

Here are some considerations:

- Are you asking God to give you peace, despite that He says He has given you His peace (John 14:27), and He says He will keep in perfect peace those whose minds are set on Him (Isaiah 26:3)? Has He told you how to have peace? Just a thought, if you don't have peace about something, maybe you're not supposed to?

- God says to hate evil (Romans 12:9, Psalms 97:10, Proverbs 8:13, Amos 5:15). People say that they struggle with sin in their lives and ask God to help them overcome it. In my experience, it is a lot easier to eliminate something you hate rather than something that just makes you feel guilty. I hate lying, so if I'm given a chance to lie or am tempted to, I will not. I hate it, not because it will or won't hurt someone, even if speaking truth comes at a cost. I wouldn't condemn you for lying to me, but I would certainly encourage you not to. I do not deny that some habits of sinning have higher costs, and I encourage people to take them to God. What I am referring to, is that people will more easily do what they don't hate. What evil do you refuse to hate and still ask God to help you overcome?

- When it comes to the fruit of the Spirit, are you trying to grow them in your life? The Bible is clear that our focus is to stay connected to the vine (John 15:5). The fruit grows as a result of making Him part of your life, not when you try and make it grow. Instead of your prayer being, "Lord, give me more patience," maybe your prayer should be, "Thank you, Lord, that you are with me and guiding me. Help me see as you see."

- Bless those who persecute you. Why are you asking God to send someone else to do it? Although you should have wisdom about the situation, I'm sure you can do something kind for them, even if it comes from you through someone else. Yes, we can pray and prophesy over their life, but is there something in your power that you could do? Doing something for them will probably do more good for you than for them.

- Speak to the mountain. What mountain or imagination do you want to see changed in your life, to be moved? "Lord, I pray that you would heal this body," is an example of speaking to God about the mountain. "Body, be healed in Jesus' name," is an example of speaking to the mountain. "Thank you, Father, that you always hear me. Lazarus, come forth!" is an example of speaking to the mountain.

So Jesus answered and said to them, "Have faith in God. For assuredly, I say to you, whoever says to this mountain, "Be removed and be cast into the sea," and does not doubt in his heart, but believes that those things he says will be done, he will have whatever he says. - Mark 11:22-23

**'Who are you, O great mountain?
Before Zerubbabel you shall become
a plain! And he shall bring forth
the capstone With shouts of
"Grace, grace to it!"'
- Zechariah 4:7**

TEN

SAY WHAT YOU BELIEVE

Are you speaking the truth or just thoughtlessly repeating things?

~PULLING DOWN~

Do people think there is no cost to confessing what they don't believe? I am not saying they are consciously deciding to lie, but that doesn't mean they are speaking the truth.

> **If anyone among you thinks he is religious, and does not bridle his tongue but deceives his own heart, this one's religion is useless.**
> **- James 1:26**

There is a very real cost to it! This is stated clearly in Scripture. This could be anything from hindering Christ being formed in you to convincing yourself to allow a work of the devil to go unresisted. I have seen some amazing fruit in my life because I started declaring truth, not what just seemed right or thoughtlessly repeating stuff I didn't believe.

Lying lips are an abomination to the LORD,
But those who deal truthfully are His
delight. Proverbs 12:22

Are you praying, "God, be with me," as if sometimes He's not? Are you not aware He will never leave you?! Are you singing, "Create in me a clean heart," but actually believe Christ has already made you a new creation? Do you talk about being a forgiven sinner but believe you are the righteousness of God in Christ Jesus? A small rudder can turn a ship. Ask yourself this - if you were walking with Jesus, would He refer to you as a sinner saved by grace or a new creation? The old man is dead, crucified with Christ; why do you talk like he is still alive?

One massive revelation to me was that I was declaring Scriptures from the way that God interacted with people before Christ and also how He interacts with me now. David prayed, "Take not thy Holy Spirit from me" in the old covenant (Psalms 51:11), but in the new covenant, Jesus says, "I will never leave you" (Hebrews 13:5). Both are in the Bible, but one was written in the old covenant, and one was in the new. Again, create in me a clean heart (Psalms 51:10), and I **am** a new creation, old things **have** passed away (2 Corinthians 5:17). So, which do you say? What do you believe?

You should not pray and sing for God to come if you already believe He is with you. You should not pray for Him to create in you a new heart if you believe He already has. You are lying to yourself, deceiving your heart. Stop repeating what you don't believe. Settle it in your heart whether He is with you, regardless of whether you feel Him and declare that. Settle whether you are a new creation, regardless of whether you still choose to follow your old man's ways, and declare that.

Please **don't** hear what I am not saying. Please **don't** use my writing as an excuse to judge others. What I am saying, is know what **you** believe. Make sure that what is coming out of **your** mouth is what **you** actually believe in **your** heart. Don't just say things because that is what others are saying. **You** are accountable before God for every idle word you speak. Ask God to sanctify you in the truth (John 17:17) and speak that.

> ***But I say to you that for every idle word***
> ***men may speak, they will give account of it***
> ***in the day of judgment. - Matthew 12:36***

~TESTIMONY~

I have made a conscious decision to speak what I believe. Talk about taking every thought captive! It took considerable effort to stop repeating what religion taught me, replace it with what I truly believed and renew my mind.

One day, as I walked through my house, I prayed, "God, give me mercy," like He was holding it back until I really needed it. I stopped myself in my tracks and asked the question, do I really believe that God was holding out on me? I mentioned earlier that words became important to me. I'm referring to Hebrews 4:16, which says, **obtain** grace, and in the Greek, it means to take, like it was on the table if you wanted it. That's a lot different from believing as I did, that God held on to it until He thought I deserved it. Now I boldly say, "Father I take the mercy you have made available to me," and believe I have it when I pray, not when I see it, and I shall have it.

~BUILDING UP~

...but, speaking the truth in love,
may grow up in all things into Him who is
the head—Christ. - Ephesians 4:15

We need to stop saying the things we don't believe. We need to guard our hearts. Limit the stranger's voice, (hearing things contrary to the Word of God) to make and keep it strange. People can be so familiar with the stranger's voice that they will follow it, thinking that God is leading them. Making the stranger's voice strange means skipping songs, not listening to wrong preaching, not reading books that don't have sound doctrine, or reading poor translations of the Bible.

Speak what you do believe (declarations), speak when you hear something you agree with (say "amen" etc.), speak (lovingly) when you hear something you don't believe. Is it worth potential discomfort to help yourself or someone else know truth? Truth makes people free! It's your responsibility to pursue renewing your mind, which is part of why we have the Helper. Renew means to change from old to new, wrong to correct. Do you think you can renew your mind when you say and sing what you don't believe; when you choose to listen to preaching you don't believe; when you read books you don't believe?

How to keep wrong thinking alive is to keep repeating it religiously. You must take captive every thought, guard your heart, and watch how you speak, sing and pray. If you now accept that God is not in control, you will start to hear those words in a ridiculous number of songs. You will hear it in preaching and see it in books and movies. Just because it is repeated a lot (I mean a lot) does not make it the truth. It's *your* mind; you choose how quickly you renew it.

One of the biggest obstacles to renewing your mind is that it will offend those that believe as you did. Religion is largely based around people who agree to believe a certain way. If you choose to renew your mind, you will put

Did you choose to stop loving them?

yourself in a place where you will have to decide what is more important. Renewing your mind to the truth, or being conformed to religion. If the renewing of your mind offends people, ask yourself, did you choose to stop loving them or did they choose to take offence? There is a big difference.

A way to renew your mind is to repeat what you do believe. A basic example of this is declaring I will not be anxious about anything, but I give my worries to God, who meets all my needs. I confess this so that I have already declared how I will respond if I "fall" into any trial. I make a lot of declarations of what the Word says is true, whether or not it is visible yet in my life. Faith is your action when things are unseen (Hebrews 11:1).

Here's a few declarations, but I strongly encourage you to read the Word and make your own list.

- I confess that Jesus is my Lord and I am saved (Romans 10:9)

- I am forgiven (Ephesians 1:7)

- I am not condemned (Romans 8:1)

- I've been set free and I am free indeed (John 8:36)

- I forget what is behind and press on (Philippians 3:13)

- I have peace and it leads me (John 14:27, Philippians 4:7)

- I have Christ in me, and I let Him be shown in my life (Colossians 1:27)

- Just as Jesus is, so am I in this world (1 John 4:17)

- I will speak/practice the truth in love (Ephesians 4:15)

- I will do the works Christ did (John 14:12)

- I will cast out devils, I will heal the sick (Mark 16:17-18)

- The same spirit that raised Christ from the dead, lives in me (Ephesians 1:19-20)

- I am made the righteousness of God (2 Corinthians 5:21)

- My prayers are effective and avail (James 5:16)

- I am being led into all truth (John 16:13)

- And on and on

Say *what you believe!*

ELEVEN

RESIST THE DEVIL!

Are you angry with God?

~PULLING DOWN~

You might assume that shifting your understanding of who God is to exclude human experience, reasoning, and false understanding leant on, would make Him seem worse, but it's the opposite.

I am no longer trying to make everything that happens to be the will of God. Now there is a purpose to knowing His will. I used to believe in a god of my own understanding who would kill innocent children to achieve some unknowable plan. I used to think that God would do this because I believed His ways were higher than mine, and that, somehow, it was loving. If Jesus did this, would you still follow Him? Didn't Jesus only do what He saw the Father do? Did Jesus just close His eyes while the Father did all this bad stuff we blame Him for?

A lot of people say that everything happens for a reason, but sometimes that reason isn't because God willed it. When you sin, is that because God made you? When I sin, did God make me? If *my* sin hurts you, do you question why *God* would do that? Are you then reevaluating who God is by your experience? Maybe that experience happened because God allowed us to choose even when our choices were harmful. An example of this might be as simple as if someone trips you over for fun and you get hurt.

> *If my sin hurts you, do you question why God would do that?*

Is that because God wanted you to fall over? Or is it that God didn't break His Word and let that person make the choice to trip you?

Our Father is infinitely more powerful than the devil. He has already overcome him (Luke 10:18, Colossians 2:15), but defeating the devil is not all He seeks. He wants to crush the devil under our feet (Romans 16:20). It is obvious that we are required to resist and overcome him too.

People might tell you that you don't need to worry about resisting the devil if you are submitted to God; this is not what the Bible tells us.

The Bible says:

- the devil has schemes that we are to be aware of (2 Corinthians 2:11)

- to be on our guard, the devil is seeking whom he might devour (1 Peter 5:8)

- not to give him opportunity (Ephesians 4:27)

- resist him (James 4:7)

- we have power over him in Jesus' name (Luke 10:19)

- stand in your armour (Ephesians 6:13)

There is absolutely no need to have power over him unless we need to exercise it. We need to stand, knowing the Father's will, and knowing what to resist.

If you find yourself angry with God, it's an indication that you are probably trying to blame Him for something that was not His will. Don't be deceived about where the gift came from (James 1:16-17). We ask God for a fish and give reasons why we get a stone, being deceived and not resisting it.

***Do not be deceived, my beloved
brethren. Every good gift and every perfect
gift is from above, and comes down from
the Father of lights, with whom there is no
variation or shadow of turning. - James
1:16-17***

Let's reflect on how Jesus is accused of casting out the devil by the power of the devil. He said a kingdom divided can't stand. People will say that Jesus wasn't operating in the enemy's camp but will reason that the devil is in God's camp on a leash. Isn't that still a house divided? The devil is not working for God's Kingdom. God is not tempting you (James 1:13). This means methods, agendas, lies, and flaming arrows are coming against the church. The devil is trying to devour us. He is trying to prosper and prevail against God's kingdom. His schemes are to be resisted and overcome. Maybe instead of reasoning why it is loving of God to give you a stone, you should be resisting a work of the devil.

The devil is not working for God's Kingdom.

Maybe your reasoning of God helps you sleep better at night while someone else suffers, but what happens if it's you that is suffering, and you can't sleep? What if it's your child in hospital? Do you thank the Lord that, in His goodness, your child suffers according to His will?

Like someone else mentioned in the Bible, do you try to put yourself above God, claiming that you're a better father and would heal your child? God wants them healed more than you do, even more than they do. He went to the whipping post and, like the Greek word for compassion, spilled Himself so it might be fulfilled according to Isaiah that 'by His stripes you were healed.'

> ***When evening had come, they brought to
> Him many who were demon-possessed. And
> He cast out the spirits with a word, and
> healed all who were sick, that it might be
> fulfilled which was spoken by Isaiah the
> prophet, saying:
> "He Himself took our infirmities
> And bore our sicknesses."
> Matthew 8:16-17***

If you have any doubt about what Isaiah 53:5 means, what did Jesus think it meant, and what did He do trying to fulfil that? Read those verses again.

If you think you need to attribute everything to God, He becomes the target of blame when things don't go the way He wills. Instead of being your strong tower to run into, He becomes the one who is firing flaming darts at you. The devil is a thief, trying to steal your faith in God. Don't let him! What happens when the devil gets his way? Read the story of Job - he is merciless in taking all he can in a moment to make Job suffer as much as possible. How does God respond? Job ends up twice as blessed.

God is good. God is a good God, and will He not give us fish when we ask for it? I've heard it said, sometimes the devil slithers up in the grass, bites you on the heel and slithers away, leaving you to blame God. If you stop trying to reason why God would do that and ask God to help you resist, you might taste and see that the Lord is good (Psalms 34:8).

God is good, and trying to reason His will to include works of the devil, only makes His character seem worse. Don't be deceived!

~TESTIMONY~

Taking shelter in the one you believe is causing the storm, is very hard.

I believed God was good and what He was doing was good, and I was far from cursing Him and dying, but I had no idea how I could take refuge in Him. When I discovered that God was not causing the storm I was in, but was *for* me, I was able to come to Him straight away with open arms and embrace Him. I could truly say, "Thy will be done," without fearing that "Thy will" meant being murdered for an unknowable plan. I am trying to say this strongly here because this is exactly what you have if everything is "Thy will."

I remember a couple of stories where someone said God injured their knee so they wouldn't play rugby on a Sunday, and another said God pushed them off their scooter so they would draw near to Him. Honestly, do you see a Jesus who would go down to a skatepark and push kids off their scooter? How would you treat me if I did that? I doubt you would think I was a good person. No doubt God works good out of bad, but to say He is the one causing the bad, beware where that leads you! I love God more than I ever have. When opportunities arise to believe Him, I'll take it!

~BUILDING UP~

I really don't mean to sound condescending here, but it is hilarious in a bad way that in people's attempt to reason and rewrite Scripture, they only make God seem worse. This happens because they try to make a work of the devil, something that a loving God in control would do. When you realise there are other wills at play, not just God's, you begin to realise that there is a lot of stuff that happened because someone else willed it, not God. No longer am I trying to reason why a good Father would give His children a stone. God is a good Father, and when we ask for a fish, then that is what we expect to receive. If we get a stone, we know it didn't come from God. Don't be deceived; every good and perfect gift comes from above (James 1:17). What is there to be deceived about? Where things that aren't good and perfect come from, because the devil is certainly not giving you good and perfect gifts!

God has never looked so good to me, and now He is a strong tower that I can run into. Now I can rest in the shadow of His wings. I can confidently pray against bad that happens, knowing

> *What is there to be deceived about?*

that I am not praying against Him. I now know a Jesus who died on a cross two thousand plus years ago, in the hopes His whipping at the post and crucifixion might result in us being over-comers, the devil being crushed under our feet, that we would have and bring the Kingdom of God to people, and them being set free.

TWELVE

FAITH AS BIG AS A SHOVEL

Faith is a choice, not something possessed

Faith, not "the faith" as in religion, but faith that moves mountains, is what this chapter focuses on. So simply defined in Hebrews 11:1, and yet so misunderstood. This chapter is probably the most crucial to get right and discuss effectively. Something I continue to press into and grow my understanding of.

> **Now faith is the substance of things hoped for, the evidence of things not seen. -**
> **Hebrews 11:1**

This may not be classed as a stronghold that needs pulling down, but faith is definitely, severely affected as the result of another. If you get one thing from this chapter, it is that right now, you can **choose** to have faith.

- Real faith, faith that is alive, is: Choosing to know and act on who God is

- Choosing to know and act on who you are in Christ

- Choosing to act in accordance with establishing His kingdom on earth

I imagine I will likely offend some people in this next bit, but I pray you will read to the end and allow me to finish before you decide where you stand.

Like it or not, faith is a choice to know how the future will go, which will likely not sit well with you if your theology is that nothing happens apart from the will of God. Just think of it like this, if you sin, are you choosing how the future will go, or do you think that it's God's will that you sinned? God is not tempting you (James 1:13). Why are people more comfortable with the idea of planting and reaping bad things than planting and reaping good? Do you believe God is choosing what you plant? Things happen that God doesn't will. Can you, will you, choose to plant and reap good by faith?

> ***Therefore I say to you, whatever things you ask when you pray, believe that you receive them, and you will have them. Mark 11:24***

In this verse, I want you to see that 'ask' means that God is yet to provide an answer. You don't know that it is His will, yet God is telling you to believe that you receive when you ask. He is telling you to choose to believe how things will go, without His consent that they do. Faith is choosing with certainty how the future will go, and your certainty will determine the actions you make in that faith. If you have faith for something to happen that is outside the will of God, all things are possible to Him who believes, but I suggest that your level of certainty will be low, your actions will be limited, and your ability to persevere and receive what you desire will be minimised.

> *Make a choice to taste and see, not just accept what will be, will be.*

Faith is choosing to taste and see, not just accept "what will be, will be." A choice, a decision, choosing. As I did, people can go their whole lives never choosing to give anything to God. They only trust God could make their future good if He wants to, which even the devil believes. Choosing to use faith, like exercising a muscle, will strengthen your ability to persevere in it. Jesus mentions a few times "little faith" (Matthew 14:31, Matthew 17:20); this often refers to how long people's faith lasts. Do you think you could continue in untested faith very long?

Action, not just mentally agreeing, at the very least, could look like going to the supermarket, declaring, "I will not be anxious." Feeding someone who is hungry when you only have a few small fish. Speaking truth when it may be seen as hate, or it could look like going where hands need to be laid. The better you know God, the easier it is to choose to act on that knowledge of Him, and the surer the foundation on which you can stand. Whatever existence you find yourself in, you can **choose** to have faith, even if your choice is just to cry, "help!" If you don't know God very well, it is more difficult to stand or hupomonē (discussed in the next chapter), but you can still have faith. We must live a life of faith, not just hoping when something seems out of our control.

> ***For in it the righteousness of God is revealed from faith to faith; as it is written, "The just shall live by faith." - Romans 1:17***

It's likely that if you held the belief that God was in control, you may not have really exercised faith beyond receiving salvation, believing that it was His will, and believing in God's goodness despite your circumstances.

There are some key things you should know about faith.

- Without it, you can't receive salvation (Ephesians 2:8)

- Without it, you can't bring pleasure to God (Hebrews 11:6)

- With it, you can inherit the promises of God (Hebrews 6:12)

- With it, you can move mountains, and nothing will be impossible for you (Mathew 17:20)

- The just shall live by it (Romans 1:17)

It is important to understand.

If the greatest, the best, the pinnacle miracle you will ever receive is salvation, and you had enough faith for that, what makes you think a lesser miracle requires more faith?

Faith is a central part of being a follower of God and needs your understanding. When the disciples asked how to increase their faith (Luke 17:5), Jesus redirected their focus and discussed what a mustard seed of faith could do. I have heard it said that people want to believe God for a million dollars when they haven't chosen to believe Him for just ten. It's like trying to believe God to get someone out of a wheelchair when you have never believed Him to heal a sprained ankle.

Faith is not denial and optimism; it is choosing to act in accordance with who God is, despite any "fact." You can choose to say, "I have no funds in the bank," which might be factual, but the truth is, you are blessed. Your Father meets all your needs (Philippians 4:19), and He owns the cattle on a thousand hills (Psalm 50:10). Facts can change, your bank account can change, your body can change, and your employment status can change, but the truth **doesn't** change. Are you confessing truth or facts? If it's facts and they change, saying the same thing again is lying. Now what you confess has to change. If I speak truth, then I can say the same thing for eternity.

> *Are you confessing truth or facts?*

One is saying God's Word, what is the other saying?

> ***Beat your ploughshares into swords***
> ***And your pruning hooks into spears;***
> ***Let the weak say, 'I am strong.'"***
> ***Joel 3:10***

Do you say you are weak, tired, or sick? Is God asking people to lie if they were? This verse does not say, "Let the weak say they are not weak", lying and denying weakness. It is a command to say you are strong, to speak truth.

> ***Therefore I take pleasure in***
> ***infirmities, in reproaches, in needs, in***
> ***persecutions, in distresses, for Christ's sake.***
> ***For when I am weak,***
> ***then I am strong.***
> ***2 Corinthians 12:10***

The truth is...

> **I can do all things through Christ**
> **who strengthens me.**
> **Philippians 4:13**

I always have the strength I need because Christ is always in me. I am strong. The condition of our body only determines physical strength. People are considerably more than their bodies. I hold the belief that I am not my body; I have a body, but who I am is spirit, and the condition of my body has nothing to do with the strength of my spirit.

The Bible says faith comes when we hear the Word of God (Romans 10:17). It doesn't say that "faith only comes...," but faith that matters is in God's Word, in His character. This is faith on which we can stand much more firmly and persevere. The best comment I have heard on this verse is that when you hear the Word of God, faith comes to believe that Word.

I believe the Lord showed me that there was a huge confusion about faith, where people were trying to collect enough faith or make it large enough to move their mountain. God has given each of us "a" measure of faith, not "different" measures (Romans 12:3). God didn't give you less than you need. You have enough faith to believe His Word, but how well will you stand on it? Holy Spirit can make use of our faith, however tested that may be, and at times gives us gifts of faith (1 Corinthians 12:9) to get His will accomplished, but His desire is that you will live by faith, not just try and use it when you want something done. He can do abundantly more than you think. Give Him something to use.

What if there was too much dirt to move quick enough?

I remember hearing this analogy which I have adapted.

If I told you that you had faith the size of a shovel, you could move a pile of dirt, it doesn't matter how big that pile was, even mountain-sized. But what if I gave you limited time to move that dirt? You might have to call on other people with their shovels to "muck in." What if there was too much dirt to move quick enough with shovels, you might have to get someone with a dozer or larger. I would ask, where did they get a dozer from? We serve a God who gives more to those who are faithful with the small (Matthew 25:29). If you want to get a dozer, be faithful with your shovel. God said that if you sowed your mustard seed, the Word, it would grow. If you let it grow deep enough (the testing of your faith) and don't let it get choked (the cares of this world, other options), it will produce a harvest (Matthew 13:23). First comes the blade, then the head, then the full grain (Mark 4:28), and the farmer doesn't know how (Mark 4:27).

If you find yourself asking, "Do I not even have a mustard seed of faith, because if I did, the mountain should have moved?" what you are really asking is, "How do I increase my faith" (Luke 17:5). The question you should be asking is, where should I plant the seed I have, where should I put in my shovel. You may or may not be able to see a trial in your own life that requires faith, but you can choose to have faith, to "muck in" in someone else's.

The size of the promise received, the mountain moved, does not determine the size of your faith, but it should show that faith was planted. Inheriting promises is a combination of faith and perseverance (Hebrews 6:12), but people make faith the scapegoat, which takes the blame for people's unwillingness to persevere. To persevere means what you believe, your faith, doesn't change; it gets tested. If you test something, you find out if what you are looking for, is there. When you test your

IQ, you see what intelligence there is. When you test your car's brakes, you want to know if they are working. Testing your faith is the same.

The devil wants to know if you'll back down and submit to him, let him prosper unresisted, or let his gate prevail. The devil will not give up anything more than he has to. If he suspects that you are not willing to stand and persevere, that you don't believe what you say, he will test you to see what he can get away with. Don't even give him a foothold. Are you fully persuaded, steadfast and quenching the enemy's darts?

> *The devil wants to know if you'll back down.*

God showed me that people lack wisdom about taking joy in trials. We aren't supposed to be taking joy in believing that God chose to make our lives hard, don't be deceived (James 1:16). We are supposed to be taking joy in that we can test our faith. As you test your faith, like walking on ice, you find out where you can plant your feet and confidently stand as long as needed. Taste and see that the Lord is good. He is good, but how much confidence do you have in that? Have you tasted?

How to have faith: Having faith is surprisingly simple and can be described in two key steps. Faith is evidence of what is unseen (Hebrews 11:1)

Step 1 - Know what is unseen

Step 2 - Show evidence about it becoming seen

Do you lack something? Health, funds, a job, a baby, a work visa, connection with a loved one? What can't you see? What is unseen?

Do something. What are you doing, believing what is unseen will be seen? There is so much that you could do. At the very least, make your requests known. Ask. Believe you receive when you pray (Mark 11:24). Do you believe that what you have asked will come to pass? Then thank God for His provision. Is someone sick, is health unseen? Lay hands. Need funds? Give away some money. Need a job? Buy a suit. Want a baby? Well, ...buy a bassinet.

> *If you have little faith, you will have little action.*

The amount you believe, have confidence, conviction, and faith in your unseen thing becoming seen will determine your actions. If you have little faith, you will have little action. If you lack confidence in your prayers healing the sick, you may only pray once. If you taste and see that God wants people healed more than you do, that He sent Jesus to make it available, you will pray until it's done or someone quits.

Getting prayers answered is what takes effort. There is not much in the New Testament about how to get prayers answered. I think if there was a "how to" there would be two main results. One is that it would negate the need for faith; two, people would immediately get legalistic. There are some main keys, mindsets, to prayers being answered that we need to be aware of.

Only believe (Mark 5:36). We need to move towards the unseen being more believed than the seen. This can manifest in a few ways, but the key one is, do your actions align with what you believe? Faith without works is dead. No fruit comes from just believing that God could do it if He wanted. If this was the case, the devil would have himself a fruit bowl. Do you believe God shall supply all your needs? Then give to bless, or lessen someone else's lack. Declarations, confessions, and renewing your mind help with this. **Say** what you believe.

Persevere. Faith and perseverance inherit the promises. If you have the faith part sorted, don't take actions that contradict it, like saying, "I don't know why that didn't work." Now your confession is that you didn't receive when you prayed. Stand. This is the part people have the most trouble with. Read the next chapter!

Last point on this: **Live it**. The just shall live by faith. Take opportunities to believe Him. Connect with Him (prayer), Disconnect with the world (fasting). Taste and see. Know **who** your faith is in. Know Him.

And this is eternal life,
that they may know You,
the only true God, and Jesus Christ whom You
have sent. - John 17:3

I wrote a poem about this that I will share here to encourage some thought on the subject of faith...

Faith

Faith is a choice, not something possessed
Not given and held, and then used by the blessed

It's a choice to hope, to believe and to act
To demand of your future, not submit to some 'fact'

Your faith is an action, if faith is alive
And faith in the Son, is what is required

It's not just for future, it's for now, it's for here
To call forth what be not, as though it were there
Great faith, fully persuaded, steadfast and bold
Can you have great faith, if you doubt what's been told

You can't act on something you don't know to believe
Which is why faith comes when you hear what you need

Faith, put to the test, is worth more than gold
Perseverance developed, it's something you hold

Perseverance and faith, gets the promise you lack
Not quoting some scripture, or whipping your back

Don't pull back your faith, don't allow its demise
Just press in and press on and reach for your prize

So where is your faith, and how is it shown
Or are you just thankful, for faith to get home

My faith is in God, His kingdom to come
On earth as in heaven, His will to be done

My faith is a choice, to believe in the truth
To believe in my future, and believe in yours, too

THIRTEEN

HUPOMONĒ

Unwavering trust in God.

~PULLING DOWN~

Some Greek or Hebrew words just can't be replaced with an English word. Like sōzō and shalom, this is another of those words.

I have chosen to use the Greek word hupomonē[3] because translators can't seem to agree on the same English word to use, patience, steadfastness, endurance, or perseverance. What if I told you there is no difference in the English words, hot and warm? They both describe something as not cold! But not knowing the difference could mean that you get burnt. There are big differences in Greek too. From all the study I have done, I suggest the most fitting word to be perseverance, but even that

---

[3] Strong's G5281 – ὑπομονή (hoop-om-on-ay')
hupomonē: a remaining behind, a patient enduring
(Some editions of Strong's spell it hupŏmŏnē in the English)

doesn't fit exactly. I encourage you to study it for yourself.

You would probably have heard someone say they are praying for more patience in their life, or someone warning against it. This is a false religious stronghold that needs pulling down. It comes from the verses that say to pursue patience (1 Timothy 6:11) and to add it to your faith (2 Peter 1:6). But if you look at the Greek word used, hupomonē, it is very different from the word makrothumia[4], which is also translated as patience, a fruit of the spirit in Galatians 5:22. This word, hupomonē, is described in two key verses, James 1:3 and Romans 5:3, as being produced in suffering. Is that what you are praying for: suffering?

> *Is what you're praying for: suffering?*

> **My brethren, count it all joy when you fall into various trials, knowing that the testing of your faith produces patience. But let patience have its perfect work, that you may be perfect and complete, lacking nothing. - James 1:2-4**

---

[4] Strong's G3115 – μακροθυμία (mak-roth-oo-mee'-ah) makrothumia: patience, forebearance, long-suffering

That word translated as patience is hupomonē.

People sing about wanting to be broken, and the devil says, "My pleasure." The devil is more than willing to make you suffer. I believe people, without thinking, are just asking the devil to make life hard for them and then accepting any attack they get, believing that God is teaching them something. Although God can masterfully work good out of any attack, and this is one way that hupomonē is produced, it doesn't mean God is causing it.

One of the things that has really helped me in my pursuit of knowing God and the truth, is looking at the Greek and Hebrew words using a Strong's-linked Bible. This is an easy thing to do through tapping on a word in a Bible app. You can also easily see where else a word has been used. It has now made my Bible come alive to me in a whole new way. Do a word search for "saved" and look at how different words are used in different places. The point I want to get to here is how different Greek words have been translated as the same word "patience." Why is that important? Because the "patience" in 1 Timothy 6:11, is not a fruit of having the Holy Spirit in your life. This is a different thing. The Bible tells us to pursue it in 1 Timothy 6:11. It says to add it to your faith in 2 Peter 1:6. Consider it pure joy when you have the opportunity to develop it (James 1:3).

Hupomonē is maybe one of the most underrated things in the Bible, which may be why we are supposed to consider it pure joy when we are given the opportunity to develop it. You need it! Hupomonē becomes character (Romans 5:3), not something you have, but something you become. The totally amazing, yet tremendously hard thing about hupomonē, is that you get to choose whether or not to test your faith (believe God) and produce it.

> *Better to test your faith when the consequences are smaller.*

Are you choosing to test your faith? Are you considering it pure joy for the opportunity to believe God? The Lord showed me that people are opting out of their opportunities. Instead of giving God the chance to provide, they borrow. Instead of giving God the chance to heal, they go to first aid. Instead of giving God the chance to give a word of knowledge, they speak whatever sounds nice.

I think this happens because people are more willing to do what they feel they can control. It takes no faith to pop a painkiller when you have a headache, but you just gave away a chance to test your faith. We get to the point where we depend on our untested faith and try to inherit the promises in situations where we don't have control. Better to test your faith when the consequences are smaller than to "build your house on the rock in the storm."

> ***You therefore must endure hardship as a***
> ***good soldier of Jesus Christ.***
> ***2 Timothy 2:3***

As I used to believe God was in control, I took this verse to mean, "be on the ready to wear sackcloth." I thought this meant that God had to make my life hard to make me more like Jesus. I now see this very differently. When you realise that God is not subjecting you to hardship, you begin to see that He is calling you to choose to fight the war, even when there is hardship in the fighting, to **choose** to endure hardship. Do you get that? He is calling you to choose to endure hardship in fighting.

Soldiers fight in a war. What, then, is the war?

> ***For we do not wrestle against flesh and***
> ***blood, but against principalities, against***
> ***powers, against the rulers of the darkness***
> ***of this age, against spiritual hosts of***
> ***wickedness in the heavenly places.***
> ***Ephesians 6:12***

The war is against the kingdom of darkness! It's choosing to resist the devil. I am not going to break down how Christians are supposed to fight, but many people I have talked to, think like Job, that God is doing everything, so they just glorify Him while waiting for the storm to pass. Jesus rebuked even the wind and the waves. Can you think of one thing besides the lusts of your flesh that you are resisting?

Suffering produces hupomonē. We can choose to participate in the sufferings of Christ (1 Peter 4:13). For what reason was the Son of Man made manifest? To destroy the works of the devil (1 John 3:8). The point I want you to get is, yes, we can wait around to "fall" into a trial, or we can choose to endure, join the war and fight like a good soldier. What manifestation of the kingdom of darkness could you be resisting? This could be a demonic influence in someone's life; it could be sickness, poverty, imprisonment, grief, etc. Your couch, TV, woodworking, and guitar-playing might be calling, but is it a priority?

~TESTIMONY~

Do you know what happens when you realise that God is not making everything happen? You start looking for ways to **make** His will happen. You start making what you **know** is His will, happen.

I started sending people messages of encouragement and gifts, not to be an encourager, but to encourage. This is the least I could do to resist manifestations of the kingdom of darkness. Overcome evil with good (Romans 12:21). I didn't do it to get anything out of it, but it was great to see people acknowledge that they had received love, even when they didn't know who it was from and glorify their Father in heaven. God is love. Also, I ended up giving words to some people without knowing that's what I was doing.

There is much more for me to grow into. I am pressing in more and more to live and love as He did and is.

The Bible says, "Encourage one another daily," not encourage one another when God gives you a feeling that makes you do it. Even right now, I reckon you could think of someone to encourage. What would make you do it? A feeling? Love is not self-seeking, so I do it wanting nothing out of it, not even the knowledge that I succeeded.

~BUILDING UP~

So how do I define hupomonē?

Unwavering trust of who God is.

We believe Him at the start of a trial, but will that waver as time goes on? How long will you believe Him before turning to another option, assuming you have one? I am trying to believe God during the trial I am currently in, when before, I had not chosen to believe Him much at all. I have not taken the opportunities presented me; trials I have fallen into. I valued my comfort more than hupomonē. I didn't consider it pure joy to test my faith.

If you look at certain things in your life and think, "I don't need God to take care of that; that's in my control. He gave me a brain; there's banks and doctors I can call on." It's not that these things

He gave me a brain.

are necessarily wrong, it's that you had the opportunity to believe God, and you didn't.

One of the things we have done in our family, is to write "second aid cupboard" where our 'first-aid' supplies are, because it reminds us to take the opportunity to believe God first before turning to a medicine cabinet. I don't condemn you for not taking opportunities to believe God, but I am telling you to start doing it when the consequences are smaller. If you will set your heart on allowing God to produce hupomonē in any suffering you fall into, you will develop character (Romans 5:4), receive promises (2 Corinthians 12:12), obey His command (Revelation 3:10), and live by faith (Romans 1:17).

Side note: I personally believe God showed me that power working in you - the kind that enables Him to do exceedingly abundantly more than you can ask or think (Ephesians 3:20) - is less hindered, operates more freely, as you allow the testing of your faith, the development of hupomonē.

FOURTEEN

CHRIST IN YOU

Something to share indeed!

In my experience with religion, sharing Jesus is often greatly emphasised. We don't want people to go to hell - fair enough, but Christ died on the cross because He "so loved people," not, "so wanted them to avoid hell." I want my life to encourage people to invite Him to be a part of theirs, and the best way I can do that is to show Him in mine.

> ***...that the sharing of your faith may become effective by the acknowledgment of every good thing which is in you in Christ Jesus. - Philemon 1:6***

This verse is a prayer that sharing your faith will be effectual (impacting and successful) by the acknowledgement of Christ in you. There are three parts to this verse: one, that you share your faith; two, that it would be effectual; and three, that you would acknowledge

Christ in you. In my experience, people seem to condemn themselves for not sharing the gospel as much as they think they should. Perhaps they should be more concerned with acknowledging Christ in them which should impact their lives so much that there is no being ashamed of the gospel (Romans 1:16), and their sharing of that fact would be much more effectual. If Christ in you, in your life, was so good, then you would have much less difficulty telling others and sharing the good news.

God loves you; He loves me; He so loves the world that He gave His only begotten Son (John 3:16). I don't say that lightly; Jesus on the cross was not a light thing. He jealously desires to be one with you, with His people, that He tells you to pray that workers will be **cast** into the harvest (Matthew 9:38). He wants to reach people through your life (Matthew 28:19). That can look like a lot of things, including being a witness (Acts 1:8), not denying Him (Matthew 10:33), and being ready to give testimony of Him being in your life (1 Peter 3:15). This chapter is focusing on the words "in you." Christ in you (Colossians 1:27), the hope of God being displayed on the earth. The hope of it happening, are you willing to allow it to happen *through* you?

How much more of a witness would you be if people can see Christ in you, rather than you telling them they need Christ who they can't see in you? If you let Christ in you be shown, made manifest, then you can be a witness all the time, even when your mouth isn't moving. When people look at you, are they seeing the fruit of Christ in you? A lot of people can quote Ephesians 4:15, which says that by speaking the truth in love, you grow into Christ, but what does that mean to you? For me, that used to mean I should be

> *How much more of a witness would you be, if people can see Christ in you?*

willing to lovingly "Bible-bash" people if I wanted to become more like Jesus. Now I can't imagine a Jesus like that at all. Jesus went about doing good and healing all, not going around and gently Bible-bashing people. If people chose to be offended at His message (John 6:61), He looked on them lovingly, didn't change His message, shook the dust off His feet and then took the next opportunity to love, whether He got persecuted for it or not.

Are you disqualifying yourself (1 Corinthians 9:27), by focusing on speaking one thing, then living something else? I think that the NET translation of the verse Ephesians 4:15, got it more accurate with the word "practising" the truth in love. This says to me, live what you believe, get better at it, renew your mind (Romans 12:2), and let Christ be formed in you (Galatians 4:19). That will speak! That is more loving than gently Bible-bashing. That is speaking in a way much less likely to be disqualified. Can you imagine a Jesus whose words were different from His actions? Hypocrite! Who would follow that?

So, what does it mean to be Christlike, to acknowledge Christ in you, and practice the truth?

> ***"But you shall receive power when the Holy Spirit has come upon you; and you shall be witnesses to Me in Jerusalem, and in all Judea and Samaria, and to the end of the earth." - Acts 1:8***

Acts 1:8, I believe, gets quite misunderstood. People read this as Holy Spirit is on people to strengthen them to witness to others. Read it again, it is saying Holy Spirit is on us to "be" a witness, not "to" witness. Holy Spirit leads you into all truth (John 16:13) and gives you strength to live and practice the truth in love. Holy Spirit doesn't come and go when He wants you to move your mouth, He abides in you. I don't deny there are times when He makes Himself more manifest, and I want Him to, but it is as He wills. (1 Corinthians 12:11) That does not mean I wait till "He wills", to choose to serve righteousness. He is with you, for you, comforts you, leads and guides you, strengthens you to "be" a witness, and the more Christ is formed in you, the more likely you are to share that. I want to live a life that speaks of the goodness of God, not a life of telling people how good God is and them not being able to see Him when I stand in front of them. Jesus says, "If you've seen Me, you've seen the Father." I want that to be true of my life.

So, what does it mean to have Christ in you; what is the fruit of having the Holy Spirit in your life? It should look like love,

> *Holy Spirit doesn't come and go when He wants you to move your mouth.*

joy, peace, patience, kindness, goodness, faithfulness, gentleness and self-control (Galatians 5:22-23). How can you tell them they can have peace when you are just as anxious about everything as they are? How can you tell people about the joy that comes from knowing Him and then complain about everything they complain about? How can you talk about God giving you the strength to have self-control if you drink too much wine like they might do, or worse yet, say God is in control, and the devil made you do it?

We need to decide that by Christ in us, by the strength that comes from Holy Spirit, we choose not to have anything in us that wasn't in Jesus. There are definitely patterns left by the old man that you need to renew (Romans 12:2). We need to put to death the old man and his ways, which means the old-man patterns still happen. The mistake is thinking that's still who you are. You are a new creation (2 Corinthians 5:17).

When you have a thought, a pattern of the old man telling you what to do, that is an opportunity to declare that's no longer who you are, thank the Lord that you are no longer the old man, not accept the thought as still being you.

> *Don't follow the stranger's voice.*

It's like letting a stranger tell you what to do; we don't follow the stranger's voice, be it the old man or the devil. A deceptive trick of the enemy is to give you a thought, convince you that it was yours, and for you to act on it. Then he tries to condemn you and make you feel guilty about it. Take the thought captive (2 Corinthians 10:5), and don't follow the stranger's voice, or you'll be back in front of your religious leader asking him for prayer to help you overcome something that wasn't you to begin with. 'Don't follow the stranger's voice' means you *will* still hear it (John 10:5).

For sure, the devil will test you, test your faith, allow you to doubt who you now are. Do you lose your peace and allow yourself to be anxious when Christ told you not to (Philippians 4:6)? Whose voice will you follow? Do you believe God wants you to be anxious, or you wouldn't be in this mess to start with? Or do you trust Him (Proverbs 3:5) and not let your heart be troubled (John 14:1); resist the enemy (James 4:7); not give him a foothold (Ephesians 4:27); and give thanks "in" all things (1 Thessalonians 5:18)?

Before your conscience and the devil try to condemn you and make you feel guilty for anything, go to God, and thank Him that you are not condemned (Romans 8:1). Acknowledge every good thing in you (Philemon 1:6); thank the Lord that He is completing a good work in you (Philippians 1:6) and forget what is behind and press on (Philippians 3:13-14).

> *Brethren, I do not count myself to have*
> *apprehended; but one thing I do,*
> *forgetting those things which are*
> *behind and reaching forward to those*
> *things which are ahead, I press toward the*
> *goal for the prize of the upward call of God*
> *in Christ Jesus.*
> *Philippians 3:13-14*

FIFTEEN

YOU DON'T HAVE TO QUALIFY

*You just need to pick
the right master!*

~PULLING DOWN~

Religion wants to compare you with who Jesus was (is) and tell you that you could do better.

You could be more equipped, come to our training or conference and get the tools, get activated, and get inspired - which means get the feelings you need to obey God. While we should be growing into the image of Christ, stirring each other on to faith and good works, iron sharpening iron, letting Christ be formed in us and becoming as the teacher, the greatest commandment is to love God and, secondly, love people. Jesus modelled this for us.

Recently, I was putting my kids to bed when I realised that I didn't want to be a better dad, but that I wanted my kids to be loved. A better dad was a title that I couldn't even quantify. Could I pass or fail? Do I use it to compare myself with others? Does it make me a good person? Does it mean that I get to be part of a group? These are all things that are attributed to me. If you want to call me a good father, that may mean I am, or maybe I'm just better than the next guy.

The real question is, am I loving my kids?

I want to pose the question, was Jesus trying to be a better Jesus, a better Christ (Romans 15:3)? Or was He acting out of His nature, who He was, making Himself a slave to loving God and loving people? One of the main themes in religion is trying to attain an acceptable level of replicating Jesus, being a "good" Christian, but you will never achieve this goal, no matter how much you try. The enemy loves to accuse the brethren of not doing "what would Jesus do?" The truth is that you will never do enough to earn being Jesus, except accepting and receiving that once born again, you already have been made the righteousness of God in Christ (2 Corinthians 5:21). You have peace with God. You can't fail at it, you don't have to become righteous, you already are, but you should choose to live righteous. Put on the new man with his nature, and as the new man, put on, choose to serve His will. You are a slave to whom you choose to serve (Romans 6:16).

You have an opportunity to choose to make righteousness your master. I used to think I was, by default, a slave to righteousness. That my actions were whatever a slave of righteousness did. Now I see that I make righteousness my master when I choose my actions. Choosing to make myself a slave to righteousness means that I don't consult my feelings. A slave doesn't serve just when he feels like it. How would my life look if I stopped choosing to be persuaded by my feelings and just did what I believed pleased my Father?

Are you aware that you're supposed to seek first the Kingdom and His righteousness (Matthew 6:33) before you even consider your feelings or your body (Romans 4:19)? Are you willing to submit to God (James 4:7), not allowing the enemy to speak through your flesh? There may be times when the right feelings, like compassion, make us move, but personally, I find that I get few feelings for doing His will. The right feelings come when you have already determined to do the will of God, not when God really desires your obedience.

In my life of religious activities, I was always very sin-conscious and felt that self-control was the ability not to do the "don'ts." I lived my life trying not to drink too much or put the wrong things in front of my eyes, not being overly complaint-driven or impatient, etc. This was still focusing on sin. This is not being dead to sin, this is keeping it alive. Choosing to be a slave to righteousness means, regardless of sin's allure, regardless of my old man feelings, there is no "should I, shouldn't I." I am a slave; the answer is yes to righteousness! The Holy Spirit strengthens me to live by that choice, my choice.

What else is self-control for? To do the "do's." Do you know how hard it is to make yourself do things, especially when your feelings aren't on board? I find it much harder to make myself do the "do's" than stop myself from doing the "don'ts." If I now make righteousness my master, put on the new man, obey the leading of the Holy Spirit, be love, then choice made. The answer is yes! The Holy Spirit strengthens me to live by that choice, my choice.

> *Before you attempt to heal all, can you even make yourself do good?*

Make your yeses, yes and your no's, no (Matthew 5:37). What does that mean? Christ went about doing good and healing all. He made Himself a servant of all. He obeyed His Father to the point of death on a cross. Before you attempt to heal all, can you even make yourself do good? Doing good usually costs you something, be it time, energy, pride, or money. Interestingly, these all boil down to pride. Am I willing to give of myself for someone else, be it God or my neighbour? Jesus says that if we want to follow Him, it starts with denying ourselves.

***Then Jesus said to His disciples,
"If anyone desires to come after Me,
let him deny himself, take up his cross, and
follow Me."
Matthew 16:24***

There is no qualification, certificate, program conference or event that is going to "activate you" to make you a slave, but that you choose. An event may inspire this choice, but you can choose now to be obedient to righteousness and become its slave. I stir you this moment to choose to make righteousness your master.

~BUILDING UP~

When I stopped trying to be something, I became something. I became something that Christ could be shown in. When I stopped trying to become somebody that Christ could use, I became less, and He became more. When I stopped caring about being a man-pleaser, self-seeking, someone that mankind was less offended by, and started fearing God and did what He commanded in His word, regardless of how I felt or whether I felt prepared or equipped, I started being used by God.

What was prevalent in my religious past was the focus on being strong, equipped, more. God says, "love others as you love yourself," love as the person you **currently are**, not who you could be. I never seemed good enough for God to use, which led me to guilt and shame. Now I am so free because what I want, I do for others, no training required. I still pursue Christ being formed in me, but I will love others now the best way I know and make room for God to do exceedingly more.

> *I never seemed good enough for God to use.*

I'm not trying to be somebody now, I am just trying to be a vessel, a donkey that brings Jesus, and it's Jesus that people need.

Jesus was the example. He made Himself humble, chose love over pride, and chose His Father's will over His own. The Bible says Jesus didn't come to please Himself (Romans 15:3). He showed me what "greater" love was in that He laid down His life for me (John 15:13). I make Him my teacher by doing what He did and what I hear Him say. I am not a sinner trying to act like (achieve the title of) a saint. I am made the righteousness of God in Christ Jesus (2 Corinthians 5:21), and I am renewing my mind to live as I am (Romans 12:2). We need to stop saying "what would Jesus do" and debating theology about what that might be, and simply love. Practising the truth in love makes you more Christlike (Ephesians 4:15). I am not trying to get the title of a good Christian; I am trying to love as Christ loved me.

SIXTEEN

LAYING A NEW FOUNDATION

Christ being the chief cornerstone

The truth will make you free (John 8:32), not religion.

Jesus is the truth.

Why bother? Because we want to know Him, to worship Him in truth. We want His kingdom on earth as it is in heaven. We want to have everything Christ paid so dearly for, to make use of the full purpose of every drop of His blood. We want to believe and live in a way that sōzō's us and others.

We don't want worthless religion! We want religion that's pure and undefiled. Repeat what you believe. STOP deceiving your heart by repeating what you don't. Just because something seems right and is repeated, doesn't mean that it is, and it could lead to death.

I don't care what seems right to man, I want to know what **is** right. Man has so many ways they think can make God move. They may not be cutting themselves (1 Kings 18:28), but they act like He is not there and needs to come out of the bathroom. He will never leave you. He wants His power working in and through you, and that happens when you realise He is already there.

Who is in control? More importantly, do things happen that are not according to God's will? Yes! Now, His will makes sense and is not mysterious. That leaves us to ponder, can I affect whether His will happens or not? Yes! At the very least, we can truthfully pray His will **BE** done when it's not occurring. What is our responsibility and authority as ambassadors of Christ? Submit to what is God, resist what is not!

Just because something is happening, doesn't mean God is allowing it. Just because someone didn't resist until bloodshed (Hebrews 12:4), didn't make it God's will that it happened. Just because you could not cast it out, doesn't mean that God was not still wanting it out. There may be times when our understanding fails us, but that's ok, we aren't leaning on it anyway. I don't claim to have apprehended, but I don't hold on to any of my failures, I press into and reach for His victory!

We are confident in knowing His will as revealed to us in His Word, not as people think their experiences reveal it. His will is not some unknowable thing, He commands us to know it. His Word is to be believed above our understanding, our experience, and reasoning. If He said it, it is true, and I believe it.

We live His way. We do things His way. When we abide in Him, He says we will bear much fruit. We are blessed when we dwell under the shadow of His wings. Let's shift our focus to abiding in Him, not on bearing fruit. There are things the Bible says to pursue and add to our faith, but we do them out of relationship with Him, not to say, "Look at my fruit." If we cannot "cast it out," we work on our relationship with Him, not come up with our own way and teach others to do that.

We say what we believe; we speak the truth in love. We need to stop speaking

---
Let's shift our focus.

---

religious lies whether we mean to or not. We practice the truth, we live it, and that speaks. We help renew our minds by speaking the truth, not speaking some man's reasoning. If the truth makes people free, we need to stop closing our mouths in the name of "niceness."

We resist the devil. We are not unaware of His schemes. We stand on the truth until it manifests. We give the devil no foothold. When he reminds us of our past, we remind him of the cross, and his future. God has given us power over all the works of the devil; let us stop asking God to move the mountains formed against us and speak to the mountains instead.

Faith is a choice! Right now, you can believe His Word. What is unseen? What action can you take as evidence you believe that unseen things are possessed and will be seen? If you know what God says about something, it's much easier to have faith for it. Faith comes by hearing the Word of God. Give Him a chance to speak, be it waiting on Him or reading His Word.

Hupomonē, like faith, is a choice. It becomes your character and affects your likelihood of staying in faith and receiving promises. It is not something we pray and ask for, but we take joy in opportunities to choose to believe God and develop it. Choose to test your faith and develop it when the consequences are smaller, rather than trying to look for it in a storm.

Christ in you is amazing. Holy Spirit is working to show you that, to show you who you already are in Him and what you already have in Him. Be transformed. Your life becomes a witness of what Christ in you means. Give Holy Spirit something to work with, strengthen, and bring to remembrance. Abide in Him, talk with Him, read the Word, and let Him speak.

You don't have to qualify. You already are a child of God, now live like one. Love God. Once you have Christ in you, you can't become any more righteous if you tried, but you can make righteousness your master, be its slave, and live accordingly. Love people as you are, and ask Holy Spirit to help you do it effectively. Choosing to love is not a qualification. Christ laid down His life for you. Freely you have received, now freely give!

Lay your foundation on truth, and build your life on the rock.

Now, therefore, you are no longer strangers and foreigners, but fellow citizens with the saints and members of the household of God, having been built on the foundation of the apostles and prophets, Jesus Christ Himself being the chief cornerstone, in whom the whole building, being fitted together, grows into a holy temple in the Lord, in whom you also are being built together for a dwelling place of God in the Spirit.
Ephesians 2:19-22

~BUILDING UP~

So how do I live and believe now?

I love God (Matthew 22:37), praise Him (Psalms 103:1), fear Him, honour Him, thank Him, hear Him, and speak to Him. I don't deny Him. I make what matters most, **first**.

I thank Him for who He is to me (John 3:16, John 10:10), that He is with me (Matthew 28:20), for me (Romans 8:31), and in me (Colossians 1:27). I am so loved by God. I never need to try to be His son, I am His son, and He is my Father. I have peace with Him and through Him.

I thank Him that I am saved and not condemned (Romans 8:1). I thank Him that I am forgiven.

I thank the Holy Spirit for comforting me (John 14:26), showing me what I already have (1 Corinthians 2:12), and giving life to my **mortal** body (Romans 8:11).

I boldly approach the throne of grace, obtain mercy and find grace in my time of need (Hebrews 4:16). I seek the strength I need to stand in faith. Mercy is stopping the fire, grace is not getting burnt though it rages on (Daniel 3), and by faith, I receive both.

I thank Him for the good that He is working out of the bad (Romans 8:28). I may fall into stuff that God didn't will or allow, but I thank Him for making good from what the devil meant for evil.

I give Him my cares and thank Him that they are taken care of, because He cares for me (1 Peter 5:7). I know when I have given something to God because it's no longer on my mind. I thank Him for His provision of the answer.

I pray in tongues a lot because I'd rather have the Holy Spirit pray on my behalf than guess at what I think I need (Romans 8:26). One thing that I do, is whenever I am inclined to speak the facts I want changed, I speak in tongues instead.

I engage in spiritual warfare and wrestle (Ephesians 6:12) to see God's will done and pray His will be done, especially His will that is known (Ephesians 5:17). As I mentioned earlier, it is much easier to pray His will be done when you know what it is, even if you just do it.

> *He's in the room, in my flesh, so I tell the body what to do.*

I speak not to God about the mountain but instead, tell the mountain to move. When I minister healing, I know that God is on the same page wanting it done. I know that if Christ were in the room in His flesh, He would tell the body what to do. He is in the room, in my flesh, so I tell the body what to do. Just as **He is**, so **am I** in **this** world (1 John 4:17). I do not try and inform God about it and ask Him to intervene.

I pray for salvations, healings, deliverance, and prospering, knowing that it **is His will**.

I bless, and I do not curse. I pray to break every curse that I'm made aware of.

I live in a way that my actions reflect Christ in me (Colossians 1:27). I thank God that He is loving others through me. By grace, I put others before me. I won't complain about issues in my life to be justified; instead, I invite others to stand with me on God's promises.

> *I speak not to God about the mountain, but instead, tell the mountain to move.*

I discern the Lord's body when I take communion and thank Him that His body was broken for me.

I regularly confess, proclaim, and declare that I receive everything Christ paid so dearly for. There is much more that I know is available to me than entry to heaven.

I prophesy into my future scriptures that I want to be fulfilled in and through me:

- I offer my body as a living sacrifice, and my mind is being renewed (Romans 12:1-2).

- The Holy Spirit is leading me in to truth, showing me what I already have, showing me things to come, making me an effective witness... (1 Corinthians 2:12, Acts 1:8, etc.)

- I will do the works that Christ did (John 14:12)

- I will lay hands on the sick and they shall recover. I will raise the dead. I will cast out devils. I will speak in tongues (Mark 16:17-19)

- I will not be anxious (Philippians 4:6)

- And on and on that goes.

I choose to spend more time in environments that will help me pursue renewing my mind and less time in environments that will conform me. This means I am discerning about churches, preachers, songs, prophecies, books etc.

I thank Him that any failings of the above are nailed to the cross, forget what is behind, press on, and can do all things through Christ who strengthens me. God is good, and His word is true and should be believed and acted upon, even when we don't understand.

SEVENTEEN

MAY GRACE ABOUND

Be strong in grace.

I want to finish with this, that grace is not just unmerited favour (Ephesians 4:7), it is also His strength in our weakness (2 Corinthians 12:9), His ability in our inability (2 Corinthians 9:8), His provision in our lack (Philippians 4:19).

Grace is God's enablement to live as He intended us to live. The word grace is used throughout the Bible, but people's understanding of it seems limited to favour which they can't merit. I want to draw your attention to these verses.

God's Command:

2 Timothy 2:1 *Be strong in grace.*

How can you be strong in something that is un-merited? By definition, you cannot merit it. Our under-standing of grace needs to grow.

Timothy is told to stir up the gift that is in him. We need to choose to live a life that requires His strength, to live a life that gives room for Him, a need for His ability to be exercised. It takes strength to live a life that can be persecuted, to speak truth that can be labelled hate speech by those who would rather you serve the god of feelings than the God of Truth. It can take strength to persevere in ministering healing or deliverance, to inherit that promise of God. These things can take a lot of strength to stand in faith, believing His Word. From where do we get this strength?

> *I can do all things through*
> *Christ who strengthens me.*
> *Philippians 4:13*

To become strong in the gym means to keep striving towards a goal that is currently out of your reach. To try and do more than what you currently have strength for. To be strong in Grace means that we keep putting ourselves in a place where we need Him, need His strength. You want to speak in front of crowds, but you wouldn't put yourself in front of ten people, be faithful in the small; to him who has, more will be given. You want to get people out of wheelchairs, start with the sore back or whatever is in front of you. Do what makes you need God, but do something. We choose the things we do, and His grace strengthens us to do them.

Some people need God's grace to get to the supermarket, but if that is all they ever do, they won't strengthen, like only ever lifting a 1 kg dumbbell. God wants for you to be strong in grace. You cannot become strong in grace by being equipped; you become strong in grace by creating a need for Him. Live by faith, and choose to do something that needs Him. If people in the gym try to lift things far beyond their strength, they can injure themselves. This is not the case with grace, God is faithful, but we are less likely to depend on Him very well in the big stuff if we have never made room for Him in the small.

Last verse of the Bible:

***The grace of our Lord Jesus Christ
be with you all. Amen.
Revelation 22:21***

I don't think it is a coincidence that Paul, over and over, at the start or the end of his letters, prays that you may grow in grace, and here in the last verse of the Bible, written by John, is the same desire. The better your revelation is of grace, the more you want it for people, the more you ask the Father for it, and the more you make room for it in your life. Make room for His grace to be with you. This is a conscious choice, like choosing to live by faith. Making room for it means giving God a chance to speak. Make time in your day to wait on the Lord. Make your first-aid cupboard your second-aid cupboard, and give God a chance to heal. Give your cares to God and see what miracle God can work in them.

The first verse with the word grace in it: Genesis 6:8 *But Noah found grace.*

Will you find grace? Will you look for it and seek after it? Do you realise you need to find it? If you have only seen grace as something you can't merit, you probably haven't looked for it, and so you probably have never made a choice to be strong in it.

The first verse in the New Testament with grace in it:

Luke 2:40 *And the Child grew in the grace of God.*

Grace is something we can grow in. You can't grow in unmerited favour, but you can grow in creating a life that is more dependent on Him, and makes more room for Him. God wants to do life with you, but if your default position is that God gave you a brain, you'll always try to solve your own problems. No condemnation on that, but it is much easier to believe His Word in a tough situation when you have lived a life of believing His Word in less challenging trials.

Where do we find this grace that we need?

John 1:16-17 *Grace and truth came through Jesus Christ.*

Do you realise that grace is received by accepting Jesus into your life? The more you imitate Him and live as He did, the more of Him you have and the more grace you have. If Christ grew in grace as He grew into the person He was, then it makes sense that we grow in grace as we grow into the person He was.

How are we saved?

Ephesians 2:8 *For by grace you have been saved.*

This is obviously unmerited favour! You will never make yourself worthy of being saved. No work you will ever perform or not perform, no hoop you could jump through will get you saved, but to come to the knowledge of the truth that God 'so' loves you, and accept it, and I pray you do.

Find grace:

Hebrews 4:16 *Let us come to the throne of grace, ...that we may find grace.*

Let's find it! It says that there is grace to be found at the throne of grace. Let's stop limiting our understanding of grace being something we can't earn, and let's start asking for it, seeking it, and knocking on God's door to find it, be strong in it, and live in it.

Great grace:

Acts 4:33 *And great grace was upon them all.*

Prayer

I would love the opportunity to pray for you.

Our Father in heaven, as you inspired prayers recorded in Your Word, may you inspire me as I put this prayer in word. Thank you. Thank You that You love us, that You are always with us, and always hear us. Thank You for your amazing grace as we renew our minds to believe Your Word. We repent of any way we have allowed our experience, reasoning, religion, or ignorance to deceive us from believing Your Word and stop it from affecting our lives. Your Word is true, and we cooperate with it to achieve all that You sent it for. We commit to seeking out and knowing Your will. We ask for wisdom in this and believe we receive it when we pray. We thank You for wisdom and strength to know what and how to resist. Help us taste and see that You are good, taking opportunities to believe Your Word, overcome, and possess new territory. Holy Spirit, I pray that You would reveal to us what we already have in Christ. We choose to have faith for Your will and Your Kingdom to manifest through us and to us. Thank You, Jesus, for laying Your life down for us. May we increase in our understanding of the victory You won and walk with You in it.

You are blessed.

About the Author

Colin is a child of God, a husband to Kelly, and a father to a lovely daughter and three amazing sons. Born, raised and living in Hamilton, New Zealand, Colin has spent a large portion of his life helping provide worship environments for Believers to enter into. A person who, through his personal trials, has learnt the foolishness of believing man's word in place of God's Word and is now on a mission to point out to all who will listen, what God's Word actually says, and encourage people to believe that. The truth will set you free, but don't take Colin's word for it; *take God's.*